SPECTATORIAL ESSAYS

Lytton Strachey, who revolutionized the art of biography in his brilliant volumes *Queen Victoria, Elizabeth and Essex,* and *Eminent Victorians,* was born in 1880. He was educated at Trinity College, Cambridge, and he became one of that distinguished company the Bloomsbury Group, which for a generation was at the center of England's literary life. His friends and intimates included John Maynard Keynes, Virginia Woolf and Leonard Woolf, and Clive Bell and Vanessa Bell. He died in 1932.

James Strachey is the brother of Lytton Strachey.

Also by Lytton Strachey

*

QUEEN VICTORIA
EMINENT VICTORIANS
ELIZABETH AND ESSEX
BIOGRAPHICAL ESSAYS
LITERARY ESSAYS
LANDMARKS IN FRENCH LITERATURE

Spectatorial Essays

LYTTON STRACHEY

With a Preface by
JAMES STRACHEY

Harcourt, Brace & World, Inc.
New York

First American edition 1965

Library of Congress Catalog Card Number : 65-10426

Printed in Great Britain

Contents

A. HISTORY AND BIOGRAPHY

A New History of Rome (*Jan. 2, 1909*)   *page* 13
Sir Henry Wotton (*Nov. 23, 1907*)   18
The Electress Sophia (*Jan. 9, 1904*)   24
The Swan of Lichfield (*Dec. 7, 1907*)   28
Three Frenchmen in England (*May 30, 1908*)   34
Warren Hastings (*March 12, 1910*)   39
The Guides (*Aug. 15, 1908*)   46

B. SHAKESPEARE AND THE ELIZABETHANS

Shakespeare's First Editors (*June 22, 1907*)   53
Shakespeare on Johnson (*Aug. 1, 1908*)   59
King Lear (*May 23, 1908*)   66
Shakespeare's Sonnets (*Feb. 4, 1905*)   71
The Pastoral (*July 28, 1906*)   76
Bacon as a Man of Letters (*Oct. 24, 1908*)   82
The Poetry of John Donne (*Jan. 18, 1913*)   88

C. THE SEVENTEENTH CENTURY

Forgotten Poets (*Jan. 27, 1906*)   97
Milton (*July 4, 1908*)   104
French Poetry (*Dec. 21, 1907*)   109
The Age of Louis XIV (*April 11, 1908*)   115
Molière (*Oct. 26, 1907*)   121
Seventeenth-Century Criticism (*May 2, 1908*)   127
The Author of 'Hudibras' (*Feb. 6, 1909*)   132

D. LATER LITERATURE

Jonathan Swift (*Feb. 27, 1909*)   141
Alexander Pope (*Nov. 20, 1909*)   147
The Poetry of Thomson (*March 14, 1908*)   153
The Grandiloquence of Wordsworth (*May 9, 1908*)   160
Coleridge's 'Biographia Literaria' (*March 7, 1908*)   166
Macaulay's Marginalia (*Nov. 16, 1907*)   171
Dostoievsky (*Sep. 28, 1912*)   174

E. THE THEATRE

Shakespeare on the Stage (*April 25, 1908*)   183
Mr Hawtrey (*Nov. 28, 1908*)   189
Mr Granville Barker (*March 28, 1908*)   194
Coquelin (*June 27, 1908*)   198
Mr Beerbohm Tree (*Feb. 1, 1908*)   203
The Sicilians (*Feb. 29, 1908*)   208
'L'Art Administratif' (*Dec. 28, 1907*)   213

Preface

The Spectator, at the beginning of the century, was edited and owned by our cousin, St Loe Strachey. It was at that time far the most widely read of the political weeklies, with a circulation in the neighbourhood of twenty thousand copies, almost three times as large as that of any of its rivals: it was to be found—so the rumours said—on the breakfast table of every vicarage in the country. *The Spectator* was in fact something of a laughing-stock among the intelligentsia of the period, and, indeed, among the younger members of our own family, who applied the term 'spectatorial' to any particularly pompous and respectable pronouncement. At the same time we were very fond of St Loe, who was the kindest of friends and a most entertaining companion and was in many ways far from spectatorial in real life. He had, in particular, a highly romantic admiration for the Strachey family, with a quite special affection for my mother, his Aunt Janie. In consequence of this, he was very ready to give my brother Lytton—who had just finished his Cambridge career and was at a loose end after failing to get a Trinity fellowship—the opportunity of writing some reviews for *The Spectator*. The first experiment (on the Electress Sophia) appeared at the beginning of 1904—it will be found included in this volume—and, after some further sampling, the editor was so much pleased by the result that eventually, in the autumn of 1907, an arrangement was made for Lytton to write a review every week. This plan remained in force until April, 1909. The strain and nuisance of this weekly effort became too great after a while, and Lytton began to devote himself to more congenial work—his elaborate articles in the *New Quarterly*,

7

and, not long afterwards, his *Landmarks in French Literature*. Altogether he contributed over eighty articles to *The Spectator*, of which some fifty date from 1908; the last one appeared in 1914.

When, in 1921, Lytton was preparing a collection of his shorter writings for *Books and Characters*, he looked through his *Spectator* contributions and decided against including any of them; and when, after his death, I was making a similar posthumous collection for *Characters and Commentaries*, I too hesitated, and eventually included only one *Spectator* article—his last one, the second which he wrote on Dostoievsky. And in the many years which have passed since then my hesitation has continued and, in spite of demands from many directions for the publication of these reviews, I am even yet not entirely convinced that it makes sense to reprint a number of them.

What is the reason for these doubts? It is a very simple one. Though Lytton was the author of these reviews, he had a secret collaborator: an unseen hand was guiding his pen. Our cousin St Loe, agreeable and amiable as he was, was an autocratic editor. I myself was his private secretary for six years, so I can give an exact report of his system. Numbers of contributors called on him in the early part of each week: leader-writers (Harold Cox, the economist, John Buchan, the unknown journalist), Eric Parker, who wrote the nature article, the clergyman who wrote the weekly sermon, and, later in the week, the various reviewers. To all of these, indifferently, the same treatment was applied. St Loe was a tremendously fluent talker, producing floods of remarkable ideas and amusing anecdotes—many of which would have startled the vicarages. These he poured over the heads of his visitors at top speed, interlaced with detailed instructions about what was to be written in the leader, the sermon or the review concerned. The visitors had hardly a moment for breathing before they were whirled out of the room. But this was not all.

On Thursday afternoons, silent, perhaps, for the first time in the week, St Loe sat back comfortably in a chintz-covered armchair with a pencil in his hand, and read through the galley proofs of the whole of the forthcoming issue. He altered a word here and there, he scribbled a fresh sentence in the margin, he struck out a whole paragraph and replaced it by one of his own. The final outcome was that each number of *The Spectator*, from the opening paragraphs of 'News of the Week' to the final series of notes on 'Current Literature', represented St Loe's opinions, expressed St Loe's policies and, most striking of all, was written in St Loe's literary style, with his unmistakable editorial first person plural. Needless to say, nothing that appeared in the paper was signed, except in the voluminous correspondence columns.

This was the situation which Lytton had to meet. If he were to say exactly what he thought and were to say it in his normal way, the editor's pencil would make hay of his review on Thursday afternoon. Instead, he adopted the method of a pre-censorship, and this he did so successfully that editorial intrusions were rarely needed. A number of these, however, may be detected in the review on 'Bacon as a Man of Letters'. Here the internal censor had dozed and the vicarages were in danger. I have printed the passage just as it appeared in *The Spectator*, only marking with square brackets (as Lytton himself did in his own copy of the review) the editor's protective additions.

Such interventions, however, were so seldom called for that at last Lytton's trustworthiness received its highest tribute: he was appointed to the post of dramatic critic. *The Spectator*, in all its long history, had never printed an article on the theatre. But now, on November 30, 1907, the revolutionary step was taken. Very special measures had, of course, to be provided for blanketing the shock to vicarage nerves. The articles were to be signed '*Ignotus*', to insulate them from editorial responsibility. And, at the end of the first one, an explanatory note appeared: 'We hope to publish from time to time papers by "Ignotus" dealing with the theatre, but we desire to take this opportunity of pointing out that the critic in question expresses his personal views, and that we are not to be held editorially responsible for his judgments. As long as the opinions given make "*les honnêtes gens*" laugh or think'—this referred to a quotation from Molière in the article—'and are honest opinions honestly expressed, as unquestionably they will be, we shall be content to leave our readers to determine for themselves whether "Ignotus" distributes his praise and blame successfully.—ED. *Spectator*.'

My hesitations over reprinting these essays will therefore be intelligible. What can remain of the original author under the pressure of this alien power? Stylistically, quite a lot. Though an occasional first person plural crops up, scarcely an essay fails to present at least one passage foreshadowing, however timorously, the writer of *Portraits in Miniature*. And in content, Lytton had in fact a very free hand so far as literature was concerned. St Loe was far from being a philistine; and, though he might admire the poems of William Barnes and even of Henry Newbolt, he shared many of Lytton's more important tastes—a passion for the Elizabethans, and a love not only of Wordsworth but of Pope. One in particular of these essays will astonish its readers—'The Guides'. Here surely, it will be thought, is pure St Loe. But in fact, though Lytton had no sympathy with St Loe's views on religion or morals, he was not at this period completely unsympathetic to some of his political attitudes. In particular, Lytton was still—perhaps, even, till the end of his life—under the spell of the history of British India, a history in which his own ancestors on both sides had played such a prominent part. His pacifism and anti-imperialism were a later growth: for the moment he could be spectatorial himself.

James Strachey

A. History and Biography

A New History of Rome*

WHEN Livy said that he would have made Pompey win the battle of Pharsalia if the turn of the sentence had required it, he was not talking utter nonsense, but simply expressing an important truth in a highly paradoxical way —that the first duty of a great historian is to be an artist. The function of art in history is something much more profound than mere decoration; to regard it, as some writers persist in regarding it, as if it were the jam put round the pill of fact by cunning historians is to fall into grievous error; a truer analogy would be to compare it to the process of fermentation which converts a raw mass of grape-juice into a subtle and splendid wine. Uninterpreted truth is as useless as buried gold; and art is the great interpreter. It alone can unify a vast multitude of facts into a significant whole, clarifying, accentuating, suppressing, and lighting up the dark places with the torch of the imagination. More than that, it can throw over the historian's materials the glamour of a personal revelation, and display before the reader great issues and catastrophes as they appear, not to his own short sight, but to the penetrating vision of the most soaring of human spirits. That is the crowning glory of the greatest history—that of Thucydides, for instance, or Tacitus, or Gibbon; it brings us into communion with an immense intelligence, and it achieves this result through the power of art. Indeed, every history worthy of the name is, in its own way, as personal as

* *The Greatness and Decline of Rome* by Guglielmo Ferrero. Translated by Rev. H. J. Chaytor, M.A. Vol. III, 'The Fall of an Aristocracy'. Vol. IV, 'Rome and Egypt'. London: William Heinemann.

poetry, and its value ultimately depends upon the force and the quality of the character behind it. From this point of view, Signor Ferrero's work on the greatness and decline of Rome is of peculiar interest. It is the work at once of a scholar and of an artist; it is based upon foundations of the most solid erudition, and it is marked on every page by the traces of a brilliant, imaginative, and exceedingly original mind. Signor Ferrero's genius is less reflective than dramatic; the picture which he unrolls before us is crowded with vivid figures, impelled towards sinister conflicts and strange dooms, struggling now with one another, now with the culminating fury of forces far greater than themselves, to be swept at last to a common ruin; and as we look we seem to be watching one of those Elizabethan tragedies in which the wickedness and the horror are mingled with a mysterious exaltation of despair. 'Where wast thou when I laid the foundations of the earth? Declare, if thou hast understanding.' That is the text of which Signor Ferrero's history is the commentary—the text of the littleness of man. The greatest names seem to lose their lustre upon his pages; he shows us the ignorance of the wise, the weakness of the strong, the folly of the prudent, the helplessness of the well-meaning; the rest is darkness and fate.

The first two volumes of Signor Ferrero's work are devoted—after a brief introductory summary—to the career of Caesar; and the third and fourth, which have now appeared in Mr Chaytor's admirable translation, carry on the history to the establishment of the power of Augustus. The scale of the work, therefore, is unusually large. The third volume, of over three hundred pages, covers a period of only seven years, and the succeeding volume is written upon the same ample proportion. This breadth of design is all the more remarkable since the amount of original material at the disposal of the historian is extremely small. The correspondence and speeches of delivered to mask one of the most curious of political intrigues.' So far all is plain sailing; but the further question remains—what were the motives of Antony? Why did he allow himself to be persuaded to throw up the game, when he had it in his power, by destroying the forces of Octavianus, to become master, not only of Egypt, but of Rome as well? To this question Signor Ferrero has no very satisfying answer to give, because he deliberately rules out of court the one answer which, in reality, is conclusive. He speaks of Antony as being 'worn out by terrible anxieties at home, exhausted by work and pleasure, unnerved by the increasing difficulties of his policy', so that 'he eventually lost his grasp of facts, and was carried away by the keen sophisms of Cleopatra.' That, surely, is a far-fetched explanation, and Signor Ferrero himself seems to disregard it when he writes elsewhere of Antony's 'incredible blundering'. His blundering was indeed incredible if it was simply produced by the 'keen sophisms' of Cleopatra. But it ceases to be so if we adopt the one hypothesis which Signor Ferrero refuses to accept, and assume with tradition that it was not the sophisms but the charms of Cleopatra which led Antony to his ruin. There is only one thing which could have blinded a man in Antony's position so completely as we now know he actually was blinded, and that thing is passion. The world might be lost if he fled to Egypt, but it would be well lost; it would be lost with Cleopatra. Is not that the only possible explanation of what occurred? If so, Signor Ferrero's narrative, so far from discrediting the famous love-story—as he believes it does—provides us, on the contrary, with overwhelming reasons for believing it true.

January 2, 1909

Sir Henry Wotton*

NO LOVER of books who has spent an afternoon—and how could an afternoon be more profitably spent?—in exploring the library of an old country house can have failed to come across, in some corner or another, a delightful fat little volume, redolent of the seventeenth century, called *Reliquiae Wottonianae*. The book, put together by Izaak Walton, is, as the title-page explains, 'a collection of lives, letters, poems; with characters of sundry personages, and other incomparable pieces of language and art, by the curious pencil of the ever memorable Sir Henry Wotton'; and Walton's charming biography of his friend appears as an introduction. Since the days of Walton very little has been added to our knowledge of Wotton's history—a history which had its full share of the movement and romance of the most moving and romantic of all ages. To his contemporaries Wotton was doubtless chiefly known as a brilliant diplomatist; but his embassies have long since passed into oblivion, and today he is only remembered—if he is remembered at all—as the author of one or two beautiful lyrics. Mr Pearsall Smith, however, in his most interesting and valuable *Life and Letters of Sir Henry Wotton* has fully remedied this neglect. His work gives us for the first time a complete presentment of Wotton—a full-length portrait of the man, standing before us in the solidity of life, and with the background of his age behind him. His two large volumes, indeed, afford a remarkable contrast to the little old *Reliquiae*. Izaak Walton assuredly did not

* *The Life and Letters of Sir Henry Wotton* by Logan Pearsall Smith. 2 vols. Oxford: at the Clarendon Press.

belong to the school of scientific historians; his biography of Wotton, inestimable though it be as an exquisitely sympathetic piece of personal reminiscence, is full of inaccuracy, vagueness, and confusion; and the series of letters which he prints has very little pretension indeed either to completeness or to chronological order. Mr Pearsall Smith is scientific in the best sense of the word, and his wide erudition, his scrupulous exactitude, his immense and enthusiastic industry, have combined to produce a work which will serve as a permanent object-lesson to the great host of slipshod literary historians. It is at first a little difficult to realize—partly owing to the author's extreme modesty—the vast mass of new material upon which the book is based. The greater part of the letters now published for the first time have been found among the Venetian papers at the Public Record Office, where they were lying unedited and unread under the dust of three hundred years. But Mr Pearsall Smith's explorations did not stop here; he has ransacked the archives of Venice and Florence and Lucca; and he has unearthed more than one important document from among the manuscript collections of our great country houses. The result is that his book is in reality something much more than its title implies. It is not merely the 'Life and Letters' of Sir Henry Wotton; it contains, as it were, a section of Wotton's epoch—a crowded and detailed panorama of the world in which he lived and worked. In fact, Mr Smith's book and Walton's biography supplement each other perfectly. Walton, who gives us principally a picture of his friend as he was in his later years, amid the quiet retirement of Eton, has preserved all the fragrance of the subject and very few of the facts. Mr Pearsall Smith has devoted the main body of his labours to the elucidation of Wotton's active life, and a single page of his book bears witness to more research than ever came within the wildest dreams of his predecessor. And it is no small part of his achievement that his pages, in spite of the weight of learning at the back of them, are eminently readable, for they are full of stirring narrative and vivid description, and they are informed throughout with a sympathy and a distinction such as it is a rare pleasure to find.

Wotton was born in 1568—four years after the birth of Shakespeare—and he lived until the eve of the Civil Wars. Thus his life covered the whole of that great epoch in the development of England which is loosely called the 'Elizabethan' age. His youthful career was adventurous enough to go straight into an historical romance. He came of a distinguished Kentish family with diplomatic traditions, and he left Oxford to go immediately to Germany, whence, after three years' study in Heidelberg, Altdorf, and Vienna, he crossed the Alps into Italy. In those days it was unsafe for an Englishman to be seen in Rome; but Wotton was determined to take the risk. His astonishing linguistic powers enabled him to disguise himself as a German so successfully that he deceived even German travellers, and it was in this character that he boldly appeared in Rome, swaggering about with 'a mighty blue feather in a black hat' under the very nose of the Pope. He returned to England to enter the service of Essex, who was then at the height of his fortunes, and he took part in the famous expedition to Cadiz and in the disastrous Irish campaign. Essex's approaching fall led to Wotton's retirement. He returned to Italy, where he became acquainted with an English adventurer, Sir Antony Sherley, who was travelling on a diplomatic mission to the Princes of Europe from the Shah of Persia. This mysterious individual introduced Wotton to an even more remarkable personage—Ferdinand dei Medici, Grand Duke of Tuscany. Ferdinand was precisely the kind of potentate who haunts the scenes of the Elizabethan dramatists; he was a master of all the arts of intrigue, he knew the secret of every conspiracy, and he possessed the antidote to every poison. He had lately dis-

covered a plot for the assassination of James VI of Scotland,
and he now despatched Wotton on a secret embassy to his
brother Sovereign in order to reveal the hidden danger.
This, as it turned out, was the crisis in Wotton's career. He
travelled to Scotland by way of Denmark, and gained an
audience of James under the title of 'Ottavio Baldi'. The
mysterious Italian—'of high stature, brown-haired, sober,
and thoughtwise', as Elizabeth's agent described him—
delivered his message and his credentials, and then, 'after
a little pause, steps to the table and whispers the King in
his own language that he was an Englishman, beseeching
him for a more private conference with his majesty.' James
was delighted with both the message and the messenger;
and when, two years later, he came to the throne of
England, he sent for 'Ottavio Baldi', gave him a knight-
hood, and made him his Ambassador at Venice.

Wotton's Venetian employment lasted, with intervals,
for twenty years, and Mr Pearsall Smith's account of this
period of his life is perhaps the most interesting, and
certainly the most original, part of his book. Whether
Wotton's voluminous despatches have quite the value—as
literature—which his biographer somewhat enthusiasti-
cally assigns to them may be doubted; but there can be
no doubt at all as to their importance from the point of
view of the historian. Mainly with their aid, Mr Smith has
been able to reconstruct a detailed picture of the life of an
English Ambassador in the early years of the seventeenth
century. He has, moreover, thrown new light on the part
played by Wotton during an important crisis in the history
of Venice—the quarrel between the Republic and the
Pope in 1606, which nearly ended in war. Wotton's attitude was misunderstood by no less an authority than
Professor Gardiner, who imputed to the English Ambassador a lack of zeal for the Protestant cause; but Mr Pearsall
Smith has shown conclusively that if any blame attached
to Wotton, it was rather for excess of zeal than for lack of it.

He was, in fact, so anxious to give a blow to the Pope's power that he went beyond his instructions in committing James's Government to an anti-Papal policy, and received in consequence a severe snub from Cecil. He even went further, for he seems to have had dreams of converting the whole Venetian State to Protestantism—dreams which, needless to say, had no other foundation than Wotton's own sanguine cast of mind. On the whole, perhaps he was less fitted for the conduct of high negotiations than for the management of those minor affairs which made up in those days the chief part of an Ambassador's duty. There was no better hand for the pilfering of a post-bag or the kidnapping of some obnoxious foreigner; there was no one more generous in the protection of his own countrymen; above all, there was no more indefatigable purveyor of news. His despatches, though they are not always easy reading— owing partly to the complexity and obscurity of their matter, and partly to the somewhat heavy elaboration of their style—are nevertheless full of interesting information and vivid detail, of strange stories and dubious adventures, with sudden glimpses of intrigues and dungeons, of gorgeous ceremonies or midnight stabbings, or the bodies of conspirators hanging head downwards between the 'fatal pillars' of St Mark.

After all, however, Izaak Walton was doubtless right, and the true background for Sir Henry Wotton is not the bustle and glamour of Italian diplomacy, but the quietude of the cloisters of Eton. How pleasantly one can imagine the kind old Provost ending his life there in happiness, with his tobacco and his *viol de gamba* and his fishing-rod, and the occasional company of 'a religious book or friend'! His best letters were written at this period of his life, and they show us the very qualities of gentle humour and refined simplicity which shine out so clearly from the features of the charming portrait in the Provost's Lodge at Eton. Mr Pearsall Smith compares Wotton to Cowley and

Marvell and Gray and other poets of the kind, but the old Ambassador hardly falls within the category of poets. Primarily he was not a man of letters, but a man of the world, though he wrote poems and wrote them well, like the rest of his generation. He belongs to the same class to which (with so different a temperament) his collateral descendant, Lord Chesterfield, also belonged—the class of literary politicians. But though Chesterfield himself might have envied the wit which went to the making of Wotton's famous definition of an Ambassador—'an honest man sent to lie abroad for the good of his country'—Wotton's cast of mind had none of the high rigidity of the eighteenth-century Earl's. Perhaps his predominant characteristic was that of cheerfulness. His letters are nearly always gay, and one feels—one does not always feel it with good letter-writers—that he himself was even more charming than his letters. He took life lightly and calmly; he had the secret of a contentment of which illness and debt and loss of friends did not deprive him; he could linger over the current of his existence as happily as he lingered over the quiet Thames with Izaak Walton beside him. He was indeed his own model in his 'Character of a Happy Life':

'This man is freed from servile hands,
Of hope to rise, or fear to fall:
Lord of himself, though not of lands;
And having nothing, yet hath all.'

November 23, 1907

The Electress Sophia*

'BE IT Enacted and Declared . . . that the Crown and
Regal Government of the said Kingdoms of England,
France and Ireland, and of the Dominions thereunto
belonging, with the Royal State and Dignity of the said
Realms, and all Honours, Stiles, Titles, Regalities, Pre-
rogatives, Powers, Jurisdictions and Authorities to the
same belonging and appertaining, shall be, remain, and
continue to the said most Excellent Princess Sophia and
the Heirs of her Body being Protestants.' Such are the
words which, in the famous Act of Settlement, finally
secured for England the Protestant Succession and the
supremacy of Parliament, and for the house of Hanover
the British throne. The fact that 'the said most Excellent
Princess Sophia' missed by a few weeks this most magnificent of all legacies doubtless accounts for the neglect she
has met with at the hands of English historians, who have
been more intent upon the 'Heirs of her Body'; but
Dr Ward's book goes far towards remedying this neglect.
He has given a careful and interesting account of Sophia's
early life, he has sketched with discrimination the part
played by the house of Brunswick in the politics of Europe,
and he has devoted an excellent chapter to the influence of
Hanover on English parties in the reign of Anne.

Even without the series of splendid reproductions of
contemporary portraits which enlivens and adorns Dr
Ward's somewhat German style, the intrinsic interest of

*The Electress Sophia and the Hanoverian Succession by Adolphus
William Ward, Litt.D., Hon. LL.D., Master of Peterhouse, Cambridge. London: Goupil & Co.

his subject would be enough to carry the reader along. One cannot help being attracted by the fortunes of a lady who was the great-granddaughter of Mary Queen of Scots on the one hand, and of William the Silent on the other, the great-grandmother of Frederick II of Prussia, the great-aunt of the French Regent, the sister of Prince Rupert, the friend of Descartes and Leibnitz, and like her ancestor Banquo, the progenitor of a line of Kings 'that twofold balls and treble sceptres carry'. It is connections such as these, at once so high and so varied, which give to the life of Sophia its distinctive charm. She was, from her birth to her death—a crowded period of eighty-four years—always a cosmopolitan. Her strange and brilliant family, deprived of their country ten years before her birth, looked to Europe to furnish them with careers or husbands. Her brothers Rupert and Maurice found their fortune in England; Edward became a Roman Catholic, and married the famous Anne of Gonzaga, 'la Princesse Palatine'; one of her sisters became a Transylvanian Princess, another a Calvinist Abbess with a taste for philosophy. The Palatines, indeed, were cultivated beyond their age. Charles Louis, Sophia's eldest brother, did his best to lure Spinoza to the University of Heidelberg, quoted Shakespeare freely, translated and acted Ben Jonson's *Sejanus*, and, says Dr Ward, 'was so sturdy a critic as to pronounce the Spanish drama superior to the French, but the English best of all.'

Sophia herself numbered among her suitors a Portuguese grandee, an Italian Duke, and a Swedish Prince; and before she settled down as Duchess of Brunswick she had flirted with her cousin, Charles of England, and been looked at by the King of the Romans. Her correspondents were as varied as her lovers. Among them was that remarkable lady, Elizabeth Charlotte, Duchess of Orleans, who did her best to enliven her exile at the French Court by writing scurrilous letters to her aunt at Hanover. Dr Ward has not thought fit to present more than a very superficial

view of *Madame's* extraordinary character, and it would be
difficult to give any adequate illustration of the colossal
coarseness of her German wit. Yet her letters, precisely
because of her unashamed speech, throw the one light that
is needed upon that moribund society which, at Versailles,
prolonged far into its decay the *Siècle de Louis XIV*. Her
Teutonic brutality sticks at nothing, and amid the flashes
of her disgusting jokes—jokes which now seek decent concealment in a learned language—one sees corruption bare.
That the Electress shared her niece's peculiar vein is
evident from that *correspondance fort étrange*, as a French
editor calls it, which passed between the two Princesses
upon a subject calculated to make a modern reader hold
his nose. But these jests of a healthy barbarism—jests that
Smollett would have delighted in—are as different from
the civilized nastiness of the Regency as an honest guffaw
is from an insinuating leer. Versailles, it is true, was the
pattern of all the Courts of Europe, but in Germany it was
only the outward form that was imitated and admired;
at Hanover—and Hanover was a typical German principality—one still, in spite of the *Grand Monarque*, drank
beer, thought freely, and was as coarse as one liked.

Dr Ward has displayed with admirable clearness the
succession of events which brought about, gradually but
inevitably, the Act of Settlement. As is so often the case in
history, it is difficult not to see in the circumstances which
surround the Hanoverian Succession some strange Providential ruling, some prescient force guiding the affairs of
men. Sophia was the twelfth child in a family of thirteen;
her family was a Protestant family, yet by an extraordinary
chance she alone of all her brothers and sisters gave issue to
Protestant heirs. But this was not enough to bring them to
the throne of England. Sophia was the granddaughter of
James I, but the Duchess of Savoy was the granddaughter
of Charles I, and until 1696 it was always possible that a
member of the house of Savoy would be chosen by Parlia-

ment to be the successor of Anne. In that year, however, Victor Amadeus threw in his lot (for the time being) with France, and all prospect of the English inheritance was at once lost to his house. But the claims of Sophia still seemed extremely remote. On the death of Mary, William was free to marry again, and there was no reason to expect that Anne's numerous progeny would all die before her. Yet William never remarried, and the death of the Duke of Gloucester in 1700 removed the last impediment to the succession of Sophia. In the same year another death hastened on what was now in any case inevitable. Charles II of Spain, after incredible delays, expired, bequeathing the whole of his vast possessions to the grandson of Louis XIV. In an evil hour Louis accepted the testament; the War of the Spanish Succession hove violently into sight; the whole of Europe was ranged upon opposing sides, and in the following year the Act of Settlement secured to England at once the alliance of Hanover and a Protestant dynasty.

That Sophia herself never reaped what had been so miraculously sown is, perhaps, the most fitting end to the story. Lingering in Herrenhausen amongst her women and her swans, conversing with Leibnitz upon metaphysics and diplomacy, trudging daily the gravel paths about her orangery between the clipped hedges and the statues and the artificial lakes, she passed the final years of her life in retirement and in peace. She kept up to the last her interest in England, telling Toland, when over eighty, 'that she was afraid the Nation had already repented their Choice of an old Woman, but that she hop'd none of her Posterity would give them any Reason to grow weary of their Dominion.' It was a pious hope, and would she not feel, if she could look back with us over the two centuries of their rule, that it had been fulfilled?

January 9, 1904

The Swan of Lichfield*

MISS SEWARD's name is a familiar one to readers of
eighteenth-century memoirs and letters, though doubtless
in the majority of cases the familiarity does not extend
further than to the name. She appears somewhat dimly in
Boswell; she flits for a minute or two through Fanny
Burney's diary; she is mentioned more than once by
Horace Walpole, and always with a laugh. Her own
letters, published after her death, in accordance with the
directions of her will, in six bulky volumes, are certainly
not calculated to inspire a closer acquaintance; and her
collected poems—'a formidable monument of mediocrity',
which Scott found himself obliged to edit—could hardly
fail to freeze the zeal of the most intrepid explorer.
Mr E. V. Lucas, however, is endowed with an intrepidity
very much above the common—a light-hearted intrepidity, which has not only carried him successfully through
the desert of Miss Seward's writings, but has even enabled
him to bring back from his journey a collection of relics
and curiosities for which every reader will be grateful.
'The Swan of Lichfield', as her contemporary admirers
called her, belongs to that class of persons who are interesting by virtue of their very fatuity, who deserve notice
simply as colossal figures of fun. 'There never was anything
so entertaining or so dull!' Horace Walpole exclaims in
one of his letters, and the phrase fits 'the Swan' to perfection. Her endless self-complacence, her infinite affectations,
her poses and her pretensions, her unfathomable ignorance, her inconceivable lack of taste—all these qualities

*A Swan and her Friends by E. V. Lucas. London: Methuen & Co

make her either intolerable or delightful, according to
one's point of view. Mr Lucas's point of view—and none of
his readers can fail to share it—commands a wide prospect
of flourishing absurdities, disposed and variegated in such
a manner as never to distress the eye. Mr Lucas is a master
of the difficult arts of selection and suppression. He has
succeeded in crowding his pages with a multitude of
amusing details and good stories and curious pieces of
information; and he has succeeded no less in passing
lightly and tactfully over the enormous number of facts
connected with Miss Seward's history and writings which,
to use Mrs Carlyle's phrase, 'it would be interesting not to
state'.

The circle in which Miss Seward lived and moved was
made up for the most part of second-rate celebrities and
third-rate poets. It was a sentimental circle, where mutual
adoration was the rule, and 'fine writing' took the place of
common speech. Miss Seward herself was always in an
ecstasy either of feeling or of flattery, and she came in for
her full share of worship from the lips of her friends. 'As
long as the names of Garrick, of Johnson, and of Seward
shall endure,' wrote one of her admirers, 'Lichfield will
live renowned.' And another declared that

> 'The British muse brings, with triumphant aim,
> Her richest tablet, graced with Seward's name.'

Among the most ardent of her votaries was Hayley, the
once famous author of 'The Triumphs of Temper', whose
verse, if we are to believe Miss Seward, 'breathes a more
creative and original genius than even the brilliant Pope'.
The alliance of the two poets was the occasion of some
amusing lines from 'the witty and wicked pen' of Dr Man-
sel, who summarized their mutual admiration as follows:

> '*Miss Seward:* Pride of Sussex, England's glory,
>   Mr Hayley, that is you.

Mr Hayley :   Ma'am, you carry all before ye,
                Trust me, Lichfield swan, you do.
Miss Seward : Ode dramatic, epic, sonnet,
                Mr Hayley, you're divine.
Mr Hayley :   Ma'am, I'll give my word upon it,
                You yourself are—all the nine.'

Unfortunately, however, this warmth of friendship was not destined to endure. For some unexplained reason, Hayley grew cool, and Miss Seward grew cool as well. 'I feel,' she wrote, with an exquisite mixture of metaphors, 'that the silver cord of our amity is loosening at more links than one.' It was true; but the Swan was by no means unprovided with consolations. When Hayley failed her, she could always be sure of sympathy from the less dazzling genius of Mr Whalley or Mr Saville; or she could seek relief in the exercise of her 'Siddonian' powers of reading aloud bad poetry among select and titled audiences; or she could fly to the Etruscan vase at Bath-Easton, drop into it a copy of verses, and be certain of being rewarded with a myrtle crown in which to walk upon the terrace in company with Lady Miller—'Mrs Calliope Miller', Horace Walpole called her—and 'sprightly Winford' (the author of the *Hobby Horse*), and 'the Nymph of Dronfield' (the author of the *Invocation to the Comic Muse*), and even, perhaps, 'time-honoured Graves' (the author of the *Spiritual Quixote*). But Miss Seward's friends were not all poets. One of the most remarkable of her acquaintances was Thomas Day, who deserves remembrance on other scores than that of having written *Sandford and Merton*. Day was one of those queer figures who, with the spread of railroads and science and uniform education, have fled for ever from the earth; he was an eccentric—when eccentricity meant something more than the wearing of unusual waistcoats; he was a character whom one could expect to find in a novel by Smollett, and nowhere else. Having made up his mind to marry, Day decided that the wisest course he could take would be to bring up under his own supervision a small girl who should ultimately become his wife. 'Sabrina', as she was called, was thirteen years old, and her education was certainly sufficiently rigorous. But the experiment did not succeed. Sabrina's spirit, Miss Seward tells us:

'could not be armed against the dread of pain, and the appearance of danger. When he dropped melted sealing-wax upon her arms she did not endure it heroically, nor when he fired at her petticoats pistols which she believed to be charged with balls, could she help starting aside, or suppress her screams. When he tried her fidelity in secret-keeping, by telling her of well-invented dangers to himself, in which greater danger would result from its being discovered that he was *aware* of them, he once or twice detected her having imparted them to the servants, or to her play-fellows.'

Sabrina never became Day's wife, and he himself fell in love with another young lady, who treated him no less cruelly than he had treated Sabrina. She declared that she would have nothing to say to him until he could dance, fence, and ride; and the poor man went off to Lyons in order to learn these accomplishments from a French master:

'I have seen him,' wrote Lovell Edgeworth, 'stand between two boards, which reached from the ground higher than his knees: these boards were adjusted with screws, so as barely to permit him to bend his knees, and to rise up or sink down. By these means M. Huise proposed to force Mr Day's knees outward; but his screwing was in vain. He succeeded in torturing his patient; but original formation, and inveterate habit, resisted all his endeavours at personal improvement. I could not help pitying my philosophic friend, pent up in durance vile for hours together, with his feet in the stocks, a book in his hand, and contempt in his heart.'

Naturally enough, when Day returned to England the lady

would have none of him. Thomas Day, blackguard, she said, had pleased her more than Thomas Day, gentleman. In the end he married, 'in spite of her wealth and *petite* figure, both of which he disliked', a Miss Milnes, 'who was known as Minerva'.

Miss Seward herself never married: she remained faithful to the Muses; and some of Mr Lucas's most amusing excerpts are those in which the poetess appraises her fellows in the craft of letters. ' "The Ancient Mariner",' she says, 'is the greatest *quiz* of a composition I ever met with,' though she allows that 'it has very fine strokes of genius.' But she is at her best on Wordsworth:

'Surely Wordsworth must be as mad as was ever the poet Lee. Those volumes of his, which you were so good to give me, have excited, by turns, my tenderest and warm admiration, my contemptuous astonishment and disgust. The two latter rose to their utmost height while I read about his dancing daffodils, ten thousand, as he says, in high dance in the breeze beside the river, whose waves dance with them, and the poet's heart, we are told, danced too. Then he proceeds to say, that in the hours of pensive contemplation, these same capering flowers flash in his memory, and his heart, losing its cares, dances with them again. Surely if his worst foe had chosen to caricature this egotistic manufacturer of metaphysic importance upon trivial themes, he could not have done it more effectually!'

Miss Seward could not be taken in; she knew what fine writing really was, and for the best of reasons—she practised it herself. This is how she describes her sensations in front of a cage of lions at a menagerie:

'My consciousness of safety luxuriates beneath the secure view of these sublimely terrible animals, in the sound of their howl and their roar; while devout thankfulness for our climate's blessed exemptions exalts and sanctifies the gratulation of egotism.'

That is fine; but the Swan was at her best when she was sentimental:

'Ah dear Mr Whalley,' she ejaculates in one of her letters 'what a rapid, what a never till then sensation took possession of my soul! fervent, instantaneous affection rushing upon my heart for a being whom, the preceding moment, I had considered as a stranger! Involuntarily I seized his hand and burst into tears, exclaiming "Do I then indeed behold the very child of dear lost Honora?"'

One can understand well enough that Miss Seward gave Scott, with whom she corresponded, 'a most unsentimental horror for sentimental letters'. But Scott seems to have had a genuine liking for her; and that perhaps speaks more in her favour than anything else. It would be impossible to think altogether ill of anyone who was a friend of Scott's. Doubtless Miss Seward's works were the worst part of her, and she would have done well for her own reputation if, instead of leaving them in her will to be published by Constable, she had burnt them—for then she would at least have been forgotten. But

> 'The evil that men do lives after them;
>   The good is oft interred with their bones,'—

although, after all, one must not be too hard even on Miss Seward's writings, for without them we should never have had Mr Lucas's book.

December 7, 1907

Three Frenchmen in England*

THE visits of Voltaire, Montesquieu, and Rousseau to England are interesting episodes well deserving of the detailed study which Professor Churton Collins has given them in a volume the publication of which is singularly appropriate at the present moment. The subject might be treated in a variety of ways—as a series of incidents in the development of European thought, as a factor in the political histories of England and France, as an illustration of the effects of international relations on literature, or as material in the biographical study of three great men of letters. It is almost entirely from the last standpoint that Professor Collins has written his book. He has been interested chiefly in the personal side of his subject, and though of course he does not ignore the broader issues, his work is mainly valuable as an elucidation of biographical facts. The amount of new matter which he has been able to collect is not very great. One of the most remarkable features of the volume is a reproduction of the strange and moving portrait of Rousseau by Wright of Derby, painted in the year of his arrival in England; and two unpublished letters by Voltaire, written in English, are of interest, not only as additions to one of the greatest and most enthralling of correspondences, but as examples of the power of style in making itself felt even through the intractable medium of a foreign tongue. But, on the whole, Professor Collins's book must be regarded rather as a skilful and

Voltaire, Montesquieu, and Rousseau in England by J. Churton Collins, Professor of English Literature in the University of Birmingham. London: Eveleigh Nash.

accurate preparation of known facts than as a treasury of
new ones. The care and scholarship which he has accustomed his readers to expect from him are evident upon
every page; obscure sources of information—such as the
contemporary notices in the London Press—have been
drawn upon with effect; and the result is a volume at once
instructive and entertaining.

Indeed, it would be no easy matter to give even the most
superficial account of the incidents of which Professor
Collins treats without striking out some sparks of interest
and pleasure from the most jaded of readers. The name of
Voltaire is in itself sufficient to start off a whole train of
delightful associations, and to raise expectations of more.
The only pity is that, so far as his visit to England is
concerned, so much should still remain in darkness. How
glad we should be to know a little more, for instance, of
that amiable Mr Falkener in whose house at Wandsworth
Voltaire seems to have spent so much of his time! The
Bolingbrokes, Voltaire informs a friend in one of the
newly discovered letters included in the present volume,
'offered me all, their money, their house; but I refused all,
because they are lords, and I have accepted all from
Mr Falkener, because he is a single gentleman.' Falkener
was a wealthy merchant who subsequently ceased to be a
'single gentleman', becoming English Ambassador at Con-
stantinople, and it was during his occupation of this post
that Voltaire dedicated to him the tragedy of *Zaïre*. He
appears to have possessed those qualities of solidity,
independence, and calm—the curiously mingled characteristics of what can only be called a stoical epicureanism
—which were shared by so many of his countrymen in the
early years of the eighteenth century. 'I am here,' he writes
to Voltaire, 'just as you left me, neither merrier nor sadder,
nor richer nor poorer; enjoying perfect health, having
everything that renders life agreeable, without love, without avarice, without ambition, without envy; and as long

as all that lasts I shall call myself a very happy man.' It is pleasant to imagine the phlegmatic English merchant and the agitated French poet strolling together through the grounds at Wandsworth discussing life and art, politics and religion, science and the drama, while the quiet summer evenings lengthened out into the night. But, needless to say, Voltaire's life in England was not all idyllic happiness. Wherever he went, he carried with him a spirit of unappeasable excitability, which constantly drove him into the most absurd and the most discreditable predicaments, and usually ended by making the place of his abode too hot to hold him. His visit to England was no exception to the rule. It is probable that he departed under a cloud, and it is certain that his conduct in London occasionally sank to very questionable levels. But the details of his adventures are doubtful in every sense of the word, and Professor Collins has not succeeded in throwing much fresh light upon them. Perhaps the most characteristic of the incidents he relates is a story of Voltaire's conduct in a street dispute, which, trivial as it is, illustrates in a remarkable way that great man's habit of getting into sordid difficulties, and his no less singular adroitness in getting out of them. His electric energy seemed to convey itself into everyone with whom he came in contact, and he could hardly walk down the street without becoming a centre of excitement. On one occasion he was surrounded by a crowd of roughs, who threw mud at him and taunted him with being a Frenchman, upon which, with astonishing promptitude, he mounted on a stone and addressed his assailants in a speech of which the first sentence only has been preserved: 'Brave Englishmen! am I not sufficiently unhappy in not having been born among you?' Oddly enough, the harangue was completely successful, and Voltaire was eventually carried to his lodgings in triumph on the shoulders of the crowd. It is impossible to conceive of such an adventure as this overtaking the refined and aristocratic Montesquieu, whose visit to England was passed entirely among persons of the highest birth and distinction. It is true that occasionally even an English nobleman was not averse in those days from a practical joke of the roughest kind, and when the author of the *Lettres Persanes* stepped forward to meet the Duke of Montagu at Blenheim he found himself plunged head over ears in a tub of cold water which had been arranged for the occasion. But his comment upon the incident is almost English in its sobriety: 'I thought it odd, to be sure; but a traveller must take the world as it goes.' One can imagine the implacable fury which, in such circumstances, would have seized upon Voltaire.

In striking contrast with scenes of this kind is the sad story of Rousseau's English visit, which Professor Collins relates with fullness, and, on the whole, with sympathy. That the clue to this epoch of Rousseau's life, darkened as it was by terrible suspicions, by gross ingratitude, and by almost absolute unhappiness, is to be found in a monomania amounting to madness must be evident to every reader of his later works, and Professor Collins unhesitatingly accepts this view of the case. It is, however, not so easy to follow him when he asserts that the first symptoms of Rousseau's malady did not make their appearance until after his arrival in London. Many years previously, at the time of his quarrel with Grimm and Diderot, signs had disclosed themselves of a maniacal tendency precisely similar to that which brought about his quarrel with Hume. Indeed, Hume's French friends had foretold the very rupture that occurred, and Horace Walpole, writing from Paris on the eve of Rousseau's departure, expressed the wish that Hume might not repent of his attachment to one 'who contradicts and quarrels with all mankind, in order to obtain their admiration.' On the whole, it seems hardly possible to doubt that Rousseau's conduct in England was merely the development of an aberration which had become manifest at a far earlier epoch in his life. The details of that conduct are set forth with terrible clarity by Professor Collins, and those who are not already acquainted with them cannot do better than consult his narrative, though it does not make cheerful reading. One circumstance in it alone stands out almost beautifully amid the gloom of the rest—Rousseau's love of inanimate Nature. As late as 1840, Professor Collins tells us, the strange Frenchman and his companion, Thérèse Levasseur, were remembered by the villagers at Wooton. The names of 'Ross Hall' and 'Madam Zell' were still repeated among them, and some could recall the alarm with which as children they had encountered the mysterious figure 'poring on the park wall for mosses, or prying in some lonely nook for plants, clad in a long gown and belt, on his head a black velvet cap with gold tassels and a pendent top, the more terrible to them because of his taciturnity.' The fears of the children were natural enough, but to us the vision seems to bring a token of consolation. The perplexed and tortured spirit could still find rest among the simple vegetable things he loved so well—the flowers, and the mosses, and the humblest offspring of the earth.

May 30, 1908

Warren Hastings*

'LET this business end as it will,' wrote Hastings at the time of his impeachment, 'a great portion of mankind will think they judge with candour, if, unable to comprehend any part of the accusations, they acquit me, at a guess, of some, and conclude that where so much is alleged against me, much of it must be necessarily true.' The prophecy has been justified by the event, for in the popular view Hastings still is, and will probably long remain, a man of mixed motives and doubtful honesty, whose brilliant services can hardly be balanced against his unscrupulousness and hardness of heart. Mr Forrest, indeed, believes that 'the drift of opinion' has changed during the last twenty years, and that 'the load of obloquy resting on Hastings' memory has in a large degree been removed.' But the facts speak differently. Only the other day there appeared, with all the pomp of academic authority, a review of Hastings's administration in which the old calumnies of Burke and Mill, duly watered down for modern palates, were once more presented to the public. Error is always long-lived, and in the case of Hastings it is only natural that it should be, for nothing approaching a true, accurate, and exhaustive account of his work has ever been written. For some mysterious reason, one of the most enthralling and stupendous interludes in English history has been left untouched by English historians. The

*Selections from the State Papers of the Governors-General of India. Edited by G. W. Forrest, C.I.E. With Portraits and Maps. Vols. I and II: 'Warren Hastings'. Oxford: B. H. Blackwell. London: A. Constable and Co.

current biographies of Hastings are totally unscientific, and—if we except one or two valuable monographs on special points in his career, together with Mr Forrest's publications—it may be said with truth that the whole enormous mass of deeply interesting material bearing upon his administration still remains to be explored. To Mr Forrest every student of Indian history is indebted for the excellent series of Selections published by him in 1892 from the Minutes of the Supreme Council in Bengal during the period of Hastings's rule. His present volumes contain a reprint of some important and little-known tracts and State Papers by Hastings, preceded by an introduction containing an account of the principal events of the Governor-Generalship. This introduction, which is an enlarged and revised version of the preface to the Selections of 1892, and now occupies an entire volume, is of unequal merit. In its original form, as a commentary upon specific documents, it was an illuminating and judicious piece of work; as it stands at present, in the shape of an independent historical essay, it is less satisfactory. The low standard of efficiency prevalent in works on Indian history is exemplified by Mr Forrest's list of authorities. The reader is referred airily to the 'original records'; but it is clear enough that this phrase must not be taken to include the immense official and private correspondence of Hastings at the British Museum—a source which Mr Forrest has left untapped. An examination of these manuscripts would, no doubt, have carried him beyond the limits of the present work, but unfortunately a similar lack of thoroughness marks his treatment of some of the most important printed materials. It is curious to note, for instance, that Mr Forrest relies for his knowledge of the actual proceedings at the impeachment upon Debrett's *History of the Trial*—a single octavo volume summarizing as best it may the nine gigantic folios containing the original evidence. What would be said of a biographer of Welling-

ton whose acquaintance with the Despatches was limited
to what he had gathered of them from some boiled-down
abstract? Or of an historian of French society under
Louis XIV who was content to read Saint-Simon's Memoirs
in a summary of a few hundred pages? In the domain
of Indian history alone are methods of this kind freely
adopted, not only by the small fry of amateurs and
book-makers, but by serious writers of knowledge and
repute like Mr Forrest. The result in the present instance is
a book which is excellent wherever it is based on the previous researches of Mr Forrest himself, or of other writers,
but which elsewhere is of disappointingly little value.

The peculiarly dramatic nature of Hastings's career was
the result in a large measure of the important part played
in it by the personal element. This fact has indeed done
much to obscure a true comprehension of his work; for
historians, from Macaulay onwards, have been usually
more concerned with the glowing colours and vivid con-
trasts of Indian personalities than with the great movements
of peoples and policies. Hastings was a statesman in the
highest sense of the word. His final achievement can only
be measured in the wide regions of administration, of
foreign policy, of finance—in the destinies, not of a few
individuals, but of vast numbers of men. Yet it is true that
the actual course of his life's work depended in a remarkable degree upon the accidents of personal character, and
thus for a proper understanding of that work a correct view
of the quarrels and intrigues which surrounded him is
highly important. Mr Forrest's most valuable contribution
to the biography of Hastings lies in this direction. The
ceaseless, deadly, almost fiendish, animosity of Philip
Francis was the determining factor in the greater part of
Hastings's career; its influence may be traced in every
branch of his administration; and without it, in all
probability, the great impeachment would never have
taken place. In the extraordinary struggle between these

mighty protagonists, the phase which has been especially illuminated by Mr Forrest is the penultimate one—that which immediately preceded Francis's departure from India, and left Hastings, for the moment at least, the uncontrolled master of Bengal. The circumstances which led up to the famous duel are known to us almost entirely through the minutes of the Bengal Council, and Mr Forrest's examination of these enthralling records leaves nothing to be desired. His commentary and verdict may be taken as conclusive, and his narrative of the facts is admirably lucid. The dispute which precipitated the final catastrophe arose owing to the singular constitution of the Supreme Council. By his casting-vote Hastings controlled the situation, until the departure of his adherent, Barwell, threatened to throw the power into Francis's hands. Barwell, however, only returned to England on the definite understanding that Francis would not use this opportunity to interfere with Hasting's conduct of the Mahratta War. But when Barwell was once out of India Francis explained away his promises, opposed the prosecution of the war, and bade fair to destroy the masterly combinations of Hastings. That the conduct of Francis was inexcusable is now beyond a doubt. 'No impartial judge,' says Mr Forrest, 'can read the minutes of the two men without coming to the conclusion that Francis was guilty of a gross breach of faith.' To Hastings the safety of the British in India depended upon the defeat of the Mahrattas, and he was determined to secure that or perish in the attempt. Hence his celebrated minute accusing his enemy of personal treachery:

'I judge of his public conduct by my experience of his private, which I have found to be void of truth and honour. This is a severe charge, but temperately and deliberately made, from the firm persuasion that I owe this justice to the public and to myself, as the only redress to both, for artifices of which

I have been a victim, and which threatens to involve their interests with disgrace and ruin. The only redress for a fraud for which the law has made no provisions is the exposure of it.'

The duel followed, and the singular spectacle was presented of the Governor-General of India and the Senior Member of Council exchanging pistol-shots. It can hardly be doubted, however, that in the desperate position in which he was placed Hastings was justified in pushing matters to this extremity. His death would hardly have increased the difficulties of the situation; and, as the affair turned out, the issue was precisely that which was most favourable to his policy. Francis was wounded; in his absence Hastings was able to push forward the attack on the Mahrattas; and when Francis, ill and shattered, returned at last to the Council, he seemed to have lost heart. He made one or two ineffectual struggles, and then left India for ever.

Much less satisfactory is Mr Forrest's treatment of another incident of Hastings's rule—perhaps the most famous of all—the affair of the Begums of Oudh. Here we feel at once the absence of an adequate body of data behind his account. Much of the most important material for forming a true judgment on this question is to be found outside the minutes of the Bengal Council, in the parole evidence given at the impeachment, for instance, and in Hastings's private correspondence, neither of which appears to have been examined by Mr Forrest; while the great mass of evidence contained in the affidavits printed by Hastings in the appendix to his *Narrative of the Insurrection at Benares* unfortunately finds no place in these volumes, though the *Narrative* itself is given us. It is in the bulk, the variety, and the unimpeachable genuineness of the statements made in the affidavits that the proof lies of the Begums' complicity in a rebellion of which the declared object was to root the English out of India.

Mr Forrest quotes a few extracts in his introduction, but that is not enough; it is the quantity and the consistency of the evidence that are really convincing. But it is not only in matters of detail that Mr Forrest's exposition might be improved upon; his whole view of the incident lacks breadth and proportion. The problem which Hastings had to face in connexion with the Begums was not merely a financial problem, as Mr Forrest, together with most of Hastings's biographers, leads us to believe; it was not merely a question of the relief of the Company's monetary embarrassments; it was part of a much larger difficulty, a difficulty involving the whole principle of our relations with the great province of Oudh. Oudh was a powerful State, dependent, in effect, upon the English Company, and at the same time a 'buffer' between Bengal and the turbulent forces upon its north-west frontier. What was to be the attitude of the English towards this principality? The policy of Francis had been deliberately to undermine the power of the Vizier of Oudh, to reduce his government to impotence, and thus to assure the supremacy of the Company beyond the shadow of a doubt. The policy of Hastings was the exact contrary; he wished for a strong, united, efficient government in Oudh, and his conduct towards the Begums was a necessary part of this policy. The Begums—the Vizier's mother and grandmother— threatened to overturn his rule, and at a critical moment all but succeeded. So long as their power existed good government in Oudh was an impossibility; and Hastings, by insisting upon the Vizier's depriving them not only of their vast domains, but of the treasures of the State upon which they had seized, was merely carrying out a consistent and admirable line of policy. In order to carry it out it was necessary to use violence—the country, we must remember, was virtually in a condition of civil war—and violence Hastings did not hesitate to use. The precise nature of the pressure put upon the Begums' Ministers

to surrender the treasures is doubtful to this day. It is
certain that they were severely manacled, it is certain they
were *threatened* with corporal punishment; more than this
is unknown. Mr Forrest, believing it necessary to excuse
Hastings, tells us that 'for what took place' he 'at Calcutta
cannot be held responsible.' But there can be no doubt
that Hastings himself would have been the first to repudiate such a defence. Indeed, it is certain that if he had
been on the spot far severer measures would have been
employed. In an unpublished letter to Impey he advocates
the summary execution of the Begums' Ministers—the two
eunuchs who had been the principal contrivers of the
confusion in Oudh. The vindication and maintenance of
the authority of the Vizier was his dominating motive, and
it was not until this end had been accomplished that he
relaxed his hold upon the centre of disaffection. The fact
that this policy involved the liquidation of a large debt to
the Company was an additional point in its favour, but the
mainspring of Hastings's action lay elsewhere. Unfortunately the true bearings of the incident have been fatally
obscured by the rhetoric of Burke and Sheridan. Hastings's
enemies ever since have assumed that he was actuated
solely by a desire for plunder, and his friends that he was
actuated solely by a desire to restore order to the finances
of the Company. In reality his aim was far wider. In this
case, as in so many others, he has been blamed or excused
for a line of conduct the true meaning of which has never
been properly understood. His severities towards the
Begums' Ministers were the necessary result of his determination to secure peace and order to a vast number of
human beings, and it is to his honour that, having the
intelligence to understand what his duty was, he possessed
no less the courage to perform it.

March 12, 1910

The Guides *

IT was a happy thought of Colonel Younghusband's to put upon durable record the most important and exciting of the many adventures which have befallen the famous corps of Guides. His book makes no pretence at being a history; it is rather a collection of stirring anecdotes loosely strung together in chronological sequence, so that it resembles in its disorder and its variety the incidents which it describes. Perhaps the uninstructed reader would have welcomed a somewhat more precise background of information to set off the mass of details which make up the greater part of the volume. The origin of the corps is passed over very lightly, and, what is more important, the nature of its composition is nowhere clearly described. If Colonel Younghusband had explained these matters more fully, and if especially he had emphasized the importance of a combination of mutually supporting bodies of horse and foot in a single corps—a fact which can only be gathered by inference from his pages—he would have considerably increased the value of his work. But these, after all, are minor blemishes, for the real merit of Colonel Younghusband's book does not depend upon the thorough-ness of its historical structure. It is not a history, but it is something which, in its own way, is as valuable and as fascinating as any history—it is the rough material out of which history is made. When the record of the rule of the British in India comes to be written, not the least thrilling and splendid of its chapters will be that for which the

* *The Story of the Guides* by Colonel G. J. Younghusband, C.B. With illustrations. London: Macmillan & Co.

present book, and others of its kind, will serve as a
foundation. That chapter will be devoted neither to
great administrative achievements nor to great military
triumphs; it will be concerned with what may seem at first
sight to be nothing more than a series of obscure struggles
over small issues with insignificant results. But, rightly
read, it will reveal much more than that—it will add a
wide domain to what we know already of the valiancy of
the human spirit and of the ennobling forces of our race.

Superficially, Colonel Younghusband's book presents
us with a curiously savage picture—a picture of violence,
disorder, ignorance, and ferocity, which, in spite of the
vein of unflinching heroism which runs through the whole,
seems to belong to some remote barbaric period of history
rather than to the latter half of the nineteenth century. It
is a book about soldiers, so that it is only natural that it
should be full of bloodshed; but it is not the quantity of
the fighting in it that is remarkable so much as the spirit in
which this fighting was carried on. These rough tribesmen
of the frontier regions of India—Afridis, Pathans, Khut-
tuks, Sikhs, Gurkhas—whose doings, on one side or the
other, either for or against the 'Feringhis', make up the
present chronicle, cannot be classed as ordinary soldiers;
to them fighting was neither a profession nor a means of
gain; it was simply a necessary condition of life. Colonel
Younghusband's pages show us a world in which all that
is most revolting to civilized man—unceasing confusion
and the reign of force—is accepted not only as the natural
state of affairs, but as the most agreeable and the best.

This atmosphere of frank and unbridled savagery,
however, though it is the most obviously striking, is not the
most interesting characteristic of these stories of the Guides.
Their fundamental significance is far more profound—it
is the example they afford of the far-reaching and benefi-
cent effects which may be produced by the powers of
order, self-reliance, and self-control. The savage tribes

of the frontier resembled some chemical substance which only required to come into contact with an appropriate force to reveal a multitude of unexpected attributes and powers. This force was the British officer, and particularly, as Colonel Younghusband is careful to point out, the British subaltern. The great achievements of the Guides— their early services in the Sikh Wars, their memorable march to Delhi, their supreme loyalty in the massacre at Kabul, and, more lately, their courage and devotion during the relief of Chitral and the fighting in the Malakand—all these things are instances of the way in which the wildest barbarism may be converted into the noblest virtue and the highest heroism. There is the shrewdness of the savage in the Pathan saying: 'First comes one Englishman, as a traveller, or for *shikar* (sport); then come two and make a map; then comes an army and takes the country. It is better, therefore, to kill the first Englishman.' But when the same savage has experienced the rule of the Englishman, when he has entered the Guides and learnt the lessons of discipline and honour, his verdict is very different. Of all Colonel Younghusband's stories perhaps the most delightful is that of Ditawur Khan, the Khuttuk bandit, who, after many years of hostility to the English, was persuaded by Lumsden to join the Guides, and remained ever after a faithful servant of his old enemies. Many years after his enlistment he confessed to Lumsden what his motives had been:

'All I took on for was to learn your tricks and strategy, and how British troops were trained, and how they made their *bandobust* for war. Directly I had learnt these things I had intended walking off whence I came, to use my knowledge against my enemies. But by the kindness of God I soon learnt what clean and straight people the sahibs are, dealing fairly by all, and devoid of intrigue and underhand dealing. So I stopped on, and here I am, my beard growing white in the service of the Queen of England.'

The central feature of all these stories is the sentiment of loyalty which they reveal. Sometimes, indeed, this feeling is carried to absurd lengths, as in the case of the orderly who, having observed that Sir John Lawrence, then Lieutenant-Governor of the Punjab, had spoken sharply to Lumsden, and that Lumsden had resented it, addressed his Colonel thus:

'I and my comrades noticed that the Lord Sahib spoke to-day words that were not pleasing to your Excellency, and that you were angry and displeased when you heard them. So we have consulted together as to how best we may serve the proper end; for it is not right and proper that we should allow our Colonel Sahib to be harshly spoken to by anyone. There is, therefore, this alternative: the Lord Sahib has arranged to leave by the straight road tomorrow morning for Peshawur, but with your honour's kind permission, and by the Grace of God, there is no reason whatever why he should ever reach it.'

It was another manifestation of the same spirit which, in the Residency at Kabul, earned for a small detachment of the Guides a splendid immortality. When the four Englishmen, whose bodyguard they formed, were massacred, the fanatic multitudes surrounding the Residency were ready to spare the lives of their kinsmen. 'The Sahibs gave us this duty to perform,' said Jemadar Jewared Singh to his comrades, 'to defend this Residency to the last. Shall we then disgrace the cloth we wear by disobeying their orders now they are dead? . . . I for one prefer to die fighting for duty and the fame of the Guides, and they that will do likewise, follow me.' They were killed to a man; and their heroism has been commemorated on the monument at Mardan, with its inscription: 'The annals of no army and no regiment can show a brighter record of devoted bravery than has been achieved by this small band of Guides.'

August 15, 1908

B. Shakespeare and the Elizabethans

Shakespeare's First Editors*

'Did some more sober critic come abroad,
If wrong, I smiled; if right, I kissed the rod.
Pains, reading, study, are their just pretence,
And all they want is spirit, taste, and sense.
Commas and points they put exactly right,
And 'twere a sin to rob them of their mite.
Yet ne'er a sprig of laurel graced these ribbalds,
From slashing Bentley down to piddling Tibbalds.
Each wight, who reads not, and but scans and spells,
Each word-catcher, that lives on syllables,
Ev'n such small critics some regard may claim,
Preserved in Milton's or in Shakespeare's name.
Pretty! in amber to observe the forms
Of hairs, or straws, or dirt, or grubs, or worms!
The things we know are neither rich nor rare,
But wonder how the devil they got there.'

OF ALL those who are acquainted with these famous lines of Pope, how many could give any satisfactory account of the 'Tibbald' (or, to use the correct spelling, 'Theobald') whom the great satirist has gibbeted with such acrimonious gusto, 'for the hand of Time to point a slow and moving finger at'? The fame of Bentley has risen superior not only to the onslaughts of Atterbury and the laughter of Pope; it has even outlived the unhappy renown of his own edition of 'Paradise Lost'. But who remembers Theobald, save as the dull commentator whom Pope

The First Editors of Shakespeare (Pope and Theobald): the Story of the First Shakespearian Controversy and of the Earliest Attempts at Establishing a Critical Text of Shakespeare by Thomas R. Lounsbury, L.H.D., LL.D., Professor of English in Yale University. London: David Nutt.

compared to dirt in amber, and who was once the hero of the 'Dunciad', until he was replaced in that honourable position by Colley Cibber? Indeed, the amber which preserves Theobald's memory now is not the verse of Shakespeare; it is the verse of Pope. To the great majority of readers it is of little consequence whether Theobald did or did not 'crucify poor Shakespeare once a week'; what *is* of consequence is that Pope said so.

Yet there can be no doubt that this view of Theobald is a totally unjust one. Professor Lounsbury, in a work which forms an elaborate and crushing commentary to the lines of Pope quoted above, has shown not only that Theobald was the victim of a malignant and unscrupulous adversary, but that there has never been a scholar to whom the ordinary English reader owes a deeper debt of gratitude. The eminence of Theobald's genius was recognized by the editors of *The Cambridge Shakespeare*, and it has supplied the subject for an illuminating essay by Professor Churton Collins; but these notices were brief and necessarily incomplete. Professor Lounsbury's monograph contains a detailed study of all the questions bearing upon this earliest of 'Shakespearian controversies'; it is based upon much learning, and upon much careful and intricate research; it is full of matter expressed with clarity and ease. The result is a book which deserves the attention of everyone interested in the history of English literature.

Professor Lounsbury's subject naturally falls into two parts—a discussion of the merits of Theobald as a Shakespeare commentator, and an account of the long, complicated, bitter, and successful campaign waged against him by Pope. Either of these topics taken separately would have afforded sufficient materials for a volume; but Professor Lounsbury has wisely blended them together, thus adding greatly to the interest of his book, though its apparent unity has been somewhat impaired. It is a little difficult at first sight to trace, for instance, the connexion between the printers of the various editions of the 'Dunciad'—the mysterious Dob, Dod, and Dodd, upon whom Professor Lounsbury is able to throw so penetrating a light—and the textual triumphs of Lewis Theobald. But the truth is that there was a very real connexion between these apparently diverse facts. Theobald's 'Shakespeare Restored' was the origin of Pope's implacable wrath; and the elaboration of the early editions of the 'Dunciad', with all their paraphernalia of mystery and subterfuge, was the machinery by means of which Pope succeeded in holding up to ridicule and scorn the greatest of Shakespearian scholars.

Nothing can give a clearer idea of the methods of criticism which Theobald's work ultimately replaced than a perusal of Pope's edition of Shakespeare, published in 1725. From many points of view it is among the most interesting of books. At the time of its publication Pope stood at the head of the profession of letters in England. He was a man of wide culture and of high intelligence; he was also a great poet. Yet as one turns over the pages of his Shakespeare it is impossible not to be appalled by the mass of ignorance, stupidity, and bad taste which it contains. It is no exaggeration to say that the meanest of journalists at the present day would be able to produce an edition of Shakespeare incomparably superior to that which the greatest man of letters of two hundred years ago spent several years of his life in compiling. And this is owing almost entirely to the change which has taken place in the conception of the meaning and function of criticism. In the days of Pope literature was something which might be measured by rigid standards and judged by immutable rules; and it was the duty of the critic to apply the recognized tests and deliver his sentence accordingly. Wretched poets were put into a bed of Procrustes, from which they rarely rose alive. It is easy enough to imagine the sort of treatment that Shakespeare received from the footrule and

the compasses of these literary surveyors. When Pope read
of 'Sleep, that knits up the ravelled sleeve of care', he
disapproved of the metaphor, and removed the line from
the text. When he came upon

> 'This my hand will rather
> The multitudinous seas incarnadine,
> Making the green one red,'

he found the language turgid, and discarded the second
line to a footnote. It is not surprising that an editor with
such conceptions of his duty should have failed to make
any careful examination of his author's text. It was not his
business to 'put commas and points exactly right', to be a
'word-catcher that lives on syllables'; his function was
simply to exercise his 'spirit, taste, and sense'. Pope made
no serious effort to collate the various editions of Shakespeare, and his elucidations of the text were nothing less
than puerile. Indeed, it is difficult for modern readers to
believe the extraordinary degree to which not only the
habits and thoughts, but the very words, of the Elizabethan
age had become unfamiliar to cultivated men in the
eighteenth century. Words which are to us neither obscure,
nor in some cases even antiquated, appeared to Pope to
be full of mystery. Such a common word as 'brooch' he
explains in one place as 'an old word signifying a jewel',
and in another as 'a chain of gold women wore formerly
about their necks'. He gravely informs his readers that
'eld' means old age, and 'gyves' shackles, and he is careful
to explain to them the meaning of 'budge'.

Theobald's edition appeared nine years after Pope's,
and at once revolutionized the study of Shakespeare. His
great achievement is that he introduced the methods of
science into literary criticism. He studied his author, not
from the point of view of theoretical art, but from the
point of view of the author himself. He became familiar
with pre-Shakespearian literature; he brought a vast fund

of erudition to bear upon the difficulties of the text; he
made a thorough collation of the various editions. But this
was not all. He combined with the scrupulous care of a
scholar the flashing insight of a genius. His brilliant and
profound emendations have restored to the world, in a
multitude of passages, the true meaning of Shakespeare.
His famous substitution in Mrs Quickly's account of
Falstaff's death of 'a babbled of green fields' for 'a table
of green fields' is remembered; but it is far from being the
only one of his corrections deserving memory. How many
of us, for instance, when we read of Macbeth's 'bank and
shoal of time', are aware that we owe the expression to
Theobald, who substituted 'shoal' for the nonsensical
'school' of the Folio? Examples of similar sagacity might
be multiplied; but two emendations mentioned by Professor Lounsbury are worthy of special notice. In the
Second Folio, and in all the subsequent editions, there is
an error in the text of *The Merry Wives of Windsor* which
till the time of Theobald had never been corrected.
Falstaff is made to say of Mrs Page that sometimes 'the
beam of her view *guided* my foot'. For 'guided' Theobald
substituted 'gilded', which in the time of Shakespeare was
frequently spelt 'guilded'. He made the alteration before
he had been able to consult the First Folio, and in the First
Folio 'guilded' is the word used. Equally remarkable was
Theobald's emendation of a well-known line in *Macbeth*,
which had appeared in every previous edition as: 'We
have *scorched* the snake, not killed it.' He read 'scotched'
(i.e., wounded) for 'scorched', and thus made sense of the
passage. The change has been universally adopted; but
modern scholarship has now shown that in Elizabethan
English the word 'scorch' was actually used as a variant of
'scotch', so that, after all, there was no need of any
emendation whatever. Yet if Theobald had never made
the alteration the sense of the passage would have been
entirely lost to many generations of readers. As Professor

Lounsbury observes, 'he comprehended what his author wanted to say, even if he did not comprehend his way of saying it.'

The later chapters of the book are devoted to an account of the process by which the reputation of Theobald gradually became obscured. The story is one of the least creditable in the annals of English scholarship. The malignity of Pope was perpetuated by the carelessness of Johnson. Warburton stole from Theobald, and insulted his memory. Capell, Stevens, Malone—all joined in the general chorus of obloquy and scorn. Thus it is not surprising to find in our own day the editor of the latest and most complete edition of Pope's works referring to Theobald as having 'no disqualification for the throne of Dullness except his insignificance'. The phrase sums up concisely enough the calumnies of two hundred years. Let us hope that Professor Lounsbury's volume may do something to redress the balance.

June 22, 1907

Shakespeare on Johnson*

IT OFTEN happens that criticism, and especially criticism of Shakespeare, is mainly interesting for the light which it throws upon the critic. This is so much the case in the delightful collection of Dr Johnson's Shakespearean work which Professor Raleigh has put together that, as every reader of it must feel, the volume would be far more correctly described by an inversion of the title. Shakespeare, for all of us, is one of those facts about which we stand in no need of comment; our relation to him—like our relation to the stars of heaven—is something quite definite, although, of course, in neither case could we express in words what that relation is. Thus the critic of Shakespeare resembles a poet who is read, not for the information which he gives us about the universe, but for his attitude towards it. As we turn over Dr Johnson's notes and prefaces we become aware that his intellect, his taste, in some sense even his character, are being brought up for judgment before a superior power. And Shakespeare's comments on Dr Johnson stand in need of no interpretation; he who runs may read. 'This play,' says Johnson, 'is one of the most pleasing of our Author's performances. The scenes are busy and various, the incidents numerous and important, the catastrophe irresistibly affecting, and the process of the action carried on with such probability, at least with such congruity to popular opinions, as tragedy requires.' The play is *Romeo and Juliet*; and who will deny that observations of that kind, while they tell us

* *Johnson on Shakespeare.* Essays and Notes Selected and Set Forth, with an Introduction by Walter Raleigh. London: Henry Frowde.

59

nothing of Shakespeare, tell us a great deal of Dr Johnson?

Undoubtedly the most abiding impression produced by the present volume is that of Johnson's eminence. Whether it is the eminence of a critic is far more open to doubt. Johnson's merits are supreme within certain boundaries; but those boundaries are narrow, and absolutely fixed. Thus it happens that when one agrees with him, it is with rapture, and when one disagrees, it is with rage. Nothing can be more 'pleasing'—to use his own expression—than to find thoughts of one's own amplified, invigorated, and brought into life in Johnson's admirable style; and nothing more exasperating than to come upon the same strength and the same clarity enforcing groundless premises or drawing absurd conclusions. The greatness of Johnson— apart from his mastery of English—lies entirely in the breadth and sanity of his outlook upon life. In this respect, as everyone knows—for who has not read Boswell?—he was unequalled, not only by the most distinguished of his contemporaries, but by very few men who ever lived. But powers of that kind—the Johnsonian largeness of vision and sobriety of temperament—though they are indispensable parts of every critic's equipment, are not sufficient in themselves to make a good critic, for the simple reason that life and literature are different things. Johnson was not, in essence, a critic of literature; he was a critic of life; and it is this fact that accounts alike for the merits and the defects of his treatment of Shakespeare. Nowhere, indeed, are the advantages of common sense and sanity in criticism more evident than among the short notes in his edition of the plays, where, as Professor Raleigh truly says, we are 'able to hear him talking without the intervention of Boswell'. When Warburton, referring to Hotspur's

> 'Methinks my moiety, north from Burton here,
> In quantity equals not one of yours,'

observes that 'Hotspur is here just such a divider as the

Irishman who made three halves; therefore, for the honour of Shakespeare, I will suppose that he wrote *portion*,' Johnson's comment is quite final: 'I will not suppose it.' In the elucidation of the text, though he was without the learning of a Theobald or a Malone, his most characteristic qualities made themselves felt to no small purpose, and Professor Raleigh in an interesting passage pays a high tribute to his powers:

'Most of the really difficult passages in Shakespeare are obscure not from the rarity of the words employed, but from the confused and rapid syntax. Johnson's strong grasp of the main thread of the discourse, his sound sense, and his wide knowledge of humanity, enable him, in a hundred passages, to go straight to Shakespeare's meaning, while the philological and antiquarian commentators kill one another in the dark, or bury all dramatic life under the far-fetched spoils of their learning. A reader of the new Variorum edition of Shakespeare soon falls into the habit, when he meets with an obscure passage, of consulting Johnson's note before the others. Whole pages of complicated dialectic and minute controversy are often rendered useless by the few brief sentences which recall the reader's attention to the main drift, or remind him of some perfectly obvious circumstance.'

In the wider field of general criticism the same qualities appear as those which enabled Johnson to triumph over difficulties of text. He refuses to be dazzled by his author. After pointing out what decency and probability require in the closing act of *All's Well that Ends Well*, he adds truly and wittily: 'Of all this Shakespeare could not be ignorant, but Shakespeare wanted to conclude his play.' And referring to the pardon of Angelo at the conclusion of *Measure for Measure*, he says with perfect justice: 'I believe every reader feels some indignation when he finds him spared.' His appreciations are often no less weighty and brilliant than his strictures. How masterly is his exposition of the

character of Polonius, with its splendid opening sentence:
'Polonius is a man bred in courts, exercised in business,
stored with observation, confident of his knowledge, proud
of his eloquence, and declining into dotage.' After Johnson
has spoken there is nothing more to be said.

But if we turn to his limitations, we find that they are no
less remarkable, and that they become obvious immediately he passes from the discussion of men and things to the
consideration of poetry. This is his verdict upon the lyrics
of Ariel: 'Ariel's lays, however seasonable and efficacious,
must be allowed to be of no supernatural dignity or
elegance; they express nothing great, nor reveal anything
above mortal discovery.' Do they not reveal a power of
evoking enchanting imaginations by means of exquisite
melody which has been discovered by very few mortals
indeed, before or since? But such a question would have
conveyed very little to Dr Johnson. His paper on *Macbeth*,
originally published in the *Rambler*, in which, by means of
'an example from Shakespeare', he indicates how poetry
may be 'debased by mean expressions', illustrates his
incapacity to judge of the propriety of words—an incapacity which he seems to have shared with most of the
critics of the eighteenth century. His judgments are
dictated merely by convention: 'knife', 'peep', and
'blanket' are 'mean expressions', and therefore Shakespeare was writing badly when he made Macbeth exclaim:

> 'Come, thick night!
> And pall thee in the dunnest smoke of hell,
> That my keen knife see not the wound it makes;
> Nor heaven peep through the blanket of the dark
> To cry, Hold! hold!'

Johnson did not understand Shakespeare's bold and
imaginative use of words; he could not see that it was in
the very expressions to which he objected that the whole

force and mystery of Macbeth's invocation lay; he completely failed, in fact, to realize the nature of the object which he believed himself to be discussing. His comparison in the 'Preface' between Shakespeare's comedy and tragedy is marked by a similar kind of misapprehension:

'In tragedy,' he says, Shakespeare 'often writes, with great appearance of toil and study, what is written at last with little felicity; but in his comick scenes, he seems to produce without labour what no labour can improve. In tragedy he is always struggling after some occasion to be comick; but in comedy he seems to repose, or to luxuriate, as in a mode of thinking congenial to his nature. In his tragick scenes there is always something wanting, but his comedy often surpasses expectation or desire. His comedy pleases by the thoughts and the language, and his tragedy for the greater part by incident and action. His tragedy seems to be skill, his comedy to be instinct.'

Is it not deplorable that the critic who can speak so finely and so sympathetically of one half of his subject should, in the very same breath, fail so utterly in his estimate of the other? 'In his tragick scenes there is always something wanting'! What was this 'something' that Dr Johnson missed? It was, no doubt, that common sense, that broad and sober view of human nature, the presence of which so delighted him in the comedies. The only 'tragick scene' which he seems to have thoroughly admired is that between Queen Katharine and her attendants in the fourth act of *Henry VIII*. This, he declares, is 'tender and pathetick, without gods, or furies, or poisons, or precipices, without the help of romantick circumstances, without improbable sallies of poetical lamentation, and without any throes of tumultuous misery.' Clearly enough, he could understand as well as any man Shakespeare's great tragic situations—the 'incident and action', as he calls it, of the tragedies. 'I am glad,' he bursts out, after his notes to the last scene of *Othello*, 'that I have ended my revisal of this dreadful scene. It is not to be endured.' And in his discussion of the conclusion of *Lear*, 'I might relate,' he says, 'that I was many years ago so shocked by Cordelia's death, that I know not whether I ever endured to read again the last scenes of the play till I undertook to revise them as an editor.' That these appalling climaxes of passion and horror moved Johnson to the very depths of his being it is impossible to doubt; but they moved him through their humanity and not their poetry. It is hardly an exaggeration to say that Johnson's criticisms are such as might have been made by a foreigner of great ability and immense experience who was acquainted with Shakespeare solely in a prose translation.

Yet, after all, though it is true that the interest of the present volume lies mainly in its revelation of the nature of Johnson's genius, it would be unfair to that great man not to confess that there is another impression which his work must produce upon the mind of every reader. The greatness of Shakespeare needs no enhancements; yet, after reading what Johnson has to tell us of him, we begin to realize that greatness more fully. Johnson sums up his judgment thus:

'This therefore is the praise of Shakespeare, that his drama is the mirrour of life; that he who has mazed his imagination, in following the phantoms which other writers raise up before him, may here be cured of his delirious extasies, by reading human sentiments in human language, by scenes from which a hermit may estimate the transactions of the world, and a confessor predict the progress of the passions.'

If this had been said by a critic of Johnson's power and experience of any other writer in the world, it would have been too high a eulogy; when it is said of Shakespeare it strikes us as completely true, but quite insufficient. Johnson has taken us up on to the vast spur of a mountain; he has measured it, he has told us of its beauties and its wonders, and he would have us believe that we have reached the topmost peak. But we can look upward, and we can still see the mighty bulk of the mountain above us, looming, inaccessible, among the clouds.

August 1, 1908

King Lear*

'THE True Chronicle History of King Leir, and his three
daughters, Gonorill, Ragan, and Cordella, as it hath bene
divers and sundry times lately acted'—so runs the
title-page of the old quarto volume containing the pre-
Shakespearean version of the famous tragedy, and now
reprinted among the interesting publications of the
Malone Society. The play is remarkable chiefly for its
extreme unlikeness to Shakespeare's. It is a good example
of the dramatic hack-work of the earlier Elizabethan
period, not without a share of the verbal felicity of the
age, showing in its verse some inevitable traces of the
influence of Marlowe, and concerned throughout with
nothing more than the telling of an old tale. Whether
Shakespeare was indebted to it at all is open to doubt; one
or two hints he may have taken from it; and, on the other
hand, it is possible that he had no knowledge of it whatever. The outlines of the plot were common literary
property; they are to be found in Holinshed, and a version
appears in *The Faerie Queen*. On the whole, it is true to say
that Shakespeare and his unknown predecessor were
working upon the same materials, so that there could
hardly be a simpler object-lesson on the meaning of genius
than that which is afforded by a comparison of *King Leir*
with *King Lear*. Ingredients which in a common vessel
will give you tolerable broth will raise immortal appari-
tions if you put them in a wizard's cauldron; and an old
wives' tale in the hands of a poetaster will remain an old

* *The History of King Leir*, 1605. The Malone Society Reprints.

wives' tale, while a Shakespeare will fill it with the rumour of the universe and all the destinies of man.

It is worthy of note that *King Lear* is, in one sense at least, a strikingly unoriginal play. To produce his stupendous results Shakespeare did not fly to new methods and dazzling inventions which had never been known before. *King Lear*, far from being the product of some gigantic *tour de force*, seems to be so naturally evolved out of the conventional fabric of the age in which it was written that it may be taken as the ideal type of an Elizabethan tragedy, just as the *Oedipus Tyrannus* is the supreme representative of the tragedy of the Greeks. Indeed, the greatest works of art appear to demand, like Kings in a procession, a train of noble forerunners to prepare their way; and genius only reaches its highest manifestations when it has, so to speak, a ready-made mould to flow into. The mould into which *King Lear* flowed was the great dramatic tradition of the Elizabethan age. All the most important characteristics of that tradition are to be found in it, wonderfully changed and heightened, it is true, but still bearing the unmistakable marks of their origin. The complexity of the plot, the general atmosphere of 'blood and thunder', the vein of high-flowing rhetoric, the presence of 'comic relief'—these are the qualities which give Elizabethan tragedies their peculiar savour, and which, often enough, are the cause of their most glaring faults. With what superb mastery has Shakespeare seized upon them, intensified them, and, at the same time, turned them to his own great uses! *King Lear*, more than any other play ever written, arouses feelings of vastness and universality; it is something more, we feel, than the history of an individual —it is the history of a world, and of a world in which, like our own, the issues are not only vital and tremendous, but multitudinous and perplexed. This impression of immense and complicated movement, which forms, as it were, the setting of the whole drama, could never have been produced if Shakespeare had not been able to employ the dramatic method of his time—to crowd his stage with a numberless succession of startling incidents, and to weave together a variety of disconnected plots into a single elaborate scheme. Modern critics have pointed out that the *dénouement* of the play is somewhat confused, and only doubtfully follows from the circumstances upon which it is supposed to turn; but the inexactitude is rather a merit than a fault, for by means of it Shakespeare—either of set purpose, or more probably by an instinctive realization of the needs of his art—gives to the events of his drama just that colouring of unexplained complexity which so often, in moments of stress and crisis, seems to belong to life itself. Here the loose logic of the Elizabethan construction helped him, and in the same way he was able to bring into his service another characteristic of his contemporaries—their promiscuity of taste. The Fool in *Lear*—that exquisite touch of irony and pathos which gives to the tragedy so strange a poignancy—has been developed straight from the comic interludes with which the earlier playwrights were wont to season their scenes of blood. Surely there could be no more marvellous instance than this of the artistic adaptation of means to ends! But Shakespeare, with the audacity of supreme genius, went further, and absorbed into the most spiritual of his tragedies the whole convention of physical violence and horror which he found reigning in the theatre when he began to write. Everyone remembers the appalling scene in which Gloucester's eyes are torn out upon the stage by Regan and Cornwall, and how many, when they think of it, exclaim with Coleridge: 'What can I say of this scene?—There is my reluctance to think Shakespeare wrong, and yet——!' But the more one reflects upon the matter, the more certain it becomes that this is a case in which it is impossible to think Shakespeare mistaken. And his justification lies in the fact that he made use of the horror of physical suffering not as an end in itself, but merely as a contributing means towards a general artistic purpose. The earlier Elizabethans show us murder and torture in order to make our flesh creep. Shakespeare shows us such things in all their terror, and then shows us something more terrific still—the inward torments of the mind. Without the experience of Gloucester's suffering we should have lacked a measure for the suffering of Lear; and when we have gauged that to its depths, when we have felt the awful revolution in that mighty soul, when we have witnessed its distraction and its ruin and its final agony, we realize that the profundities of the spirit stretch infinitely beyond the pains of the body, and we begin to think of Gloucester's blinding as of something almost insignificant.

But the superstructure which in *King Lear* Shakespeare raised upon the foundations of the Elizabethan tradition is more even than a great spiritual tragedy—it is a tragedy which in the widest sense of the term may be called universal. By a mysterious art he has conveyed into it suggestions of the vastest import; its colossal figures move upon a superhuman stage; their struggles seem in some strange way to be the struggles of humanity itself, and in their destinies are symbolized the destinies of the whole world. The picture is one of almost absolute gloom. 'In this the most terrible work of human genius,' says Mr Swinburne, 'it is with the very springs and sources of nature that her student has set himself to deal. The veil of the temple of our humanity is rent in twain. Nature herself, we might say, is revealed—and revealed as un-natural. In face of such a world as this a man might be forgiven who should pray that chaos might come again.' That is true; and yet who has ever read *King Lear* that has not, in spite of all the terror and the pity of it, in spite even of the dreadful close, found something more in his mind than despair and desolation? It is the most wonderful fact about this wonderful tragedy that it has built, in the very heart of darkness, a temple of majesty and light. It leaves us at last convinced that, somehow or other, these things, terrible as they are, have been supremely 'worth while'. After all our other feelings, is it not with one akin to triumph that we end?

May 23, 1908

Shakespeare's Sonnets*

HE IS a bold man who sets out in quest of the key which shall unlock the mystery of Shakespeare's sonnets. In that country the roads make heavy walking, and 'airy tongues that syllable men's names' lure the unwary traveller at every turn into paths already white with the bones of innumerable commentators. Yet the fascination of the search seems to outweigh its dangers, for each year adds to the number of these sanguine explorers, while it engulfs their predecessors in a deeper oblivion. Nor is it difficult to trace the sources from which the fascination of the sonnets springs. It is not only that the problem they present affords scope for the exercise of that sort of literary detective work which takes joy in tracking out, for instance, the author of the Junius Letters; there is another and more potent attraction in the mystery of the sonnets. For its solution seems to offer hopes of a prize of extraordinary value—nothing less than a true insight into the most secret recesses of the thoughts and feelings of perhaps the greatest man who ever lived. The belief that the sonnets contain the clue which leads straight into the hidden *penetralia* of Shakespeare's biography is at the root of most of the investigation that has been spent upon them.

The two volumes now before us afford excellent examples of how such an investigation ought, and ought not, to be carried on. Canon Beeching's introduction to the

*(1) *The Sonnets of Shakespeare.* With an Introduction and Notes by H. C. Beeching, M.A., D.Litt. London: Ginn & Co. (2) *Shakespeare Self-Revealed in his Sonnets, and Phoenix and Turtle.* The Texts, with an Introduction and Analyses by J. M. London: Sherratt & Hughes.

edition of the sonnets which he has prepared for the Athenaeum Press series is a scholarly and able contribution to the literature of the subject; the same cannot be said of *Shakespeare Self-Revealed*, a work whose title curiously belies its contents, more than half of its pages being devoted to the revelations, not of Shakespeare, but of 'J. M.', its anonymous editor. 'Let us now behold,' is the motto of the latter work, 'a human soul made visible in life'; but if the reference is to the soul of Shakespeare, the reader's expectation will be disappointed. He will find instead some hazy speculation, a great number of unfounded assertions, and a vast mass of heterogeneous quotations from Bacon, Thoreau, Montaigne, Ruskin, Spenser, Castiglione, Coleridge, Ben Jonson, King Solomon, Sir Leslie Stephen, and many other writers. The main thesis of the introduction—that the 'two loves' of the sonnets typify the Love of Beauty and the Love of Fame, which divided the mind of Shakespeare—is a mere assumption unsupported by a scrap of evidence, and devoid even of the merit of being interesting; and the whole treatment of the subject provides a remarkable illustration of the straits to which theory-making may be reduced when it is the facts which are fitted into the theory, and not the theory on to the facts.

Canon Beeching's essay demands more serious attention, both because of its intrinsic value, and because it contains a counterblast to a theory of the sonnets which has lately obtained wide acceptance, and has gained strong support by the advocacy of Mr Sidney Lee. That the sonnets were not the outcome of deep emotion; that they were written, not to a friend, but to a patron; and that that patron was probably the Earl of Southampton— these are the main articles in the creed of Mr Lee and his followers, and a discussion of them occupies a large part of Canon Beeching's introduction. The conclusions at which he arrives seem to be completely justified by the facts. As far as the identity of 'Mr W. H.' with Southampton is concerned, it is difficult to believe that an unbiased reader of Canon Beeching's pages will fail to see that a case of such strength has been made out against Mr Sidney Lee's position that this theory is now no longer tenable. That theory involves, as Canon Beeching shows, a 'nonnatural interpretation of words and phrases'; it raises insuperable difficulties as to the meaning of the 'Envoy'; and it necessitates an assumption as to the date of the composition of the sonnets which is not only unsupported by any evidence whatever, but is incompatible with linguistic considerations of some weight.

If, then, the claims of Southampton must be definitely ruled out of court, do those of his rival, William Herbert, Earl of Pembroke, deserve a better fate? Canon Beeching's discussion of this question is refreshingly moderate; and his conclusions are convincing. On the one hand, he clearly proves that none of the objections which have been urged against the Herbert theory are really valid; on the other, he points out that we do not possess sufficient evidence to justify a definite decision in Herbert's favour. All that can be said with certainty is that the characteristics of the 'W. H.' of the sonnets do seem to tally in a remarkable way with everything that we know of William Herbert.

Canon Beeching, in pointing out this fact, quotes the evidence of some contemporary witnesses as to the Earl's character and personal appearance, but he has omitted to refer to the passage which tells more strikingly than any other in favour of his argument—Clarendon's portrait of Pembroke in his *History of the Rebellion*. Pembroke, we there learn, was 'the most universally loved and esteemed of any man of that age.' He was 'a man very well bred, and of excellent parts, and a graceful speaker upon any subject, having a good proportion of learning, and a ready wit to apply it and enlarge upon it; of a pleasant and facetious humour, and a disposition affable, generous, and magnificent. . . . And as his conversation was most with men of the most pregnant parts and understanding, so towards any who needed support and encouragement, though unknown, if fairly recommended to him, he was very liberal.' And the judicious chronicler concludes with a passage curiously suggestive of more than one passage in the sonnets:

'Yet his memory must not be so flattered that his virtues and good inclinations may be believed without some allay of vice, and without being clouded with great infirmities, which he had in too exorbitant a proportion. He indulged to himself pleasures of all kinds, almost in all excesses. To women, whether out of his natural constitution, or for want of his domestic content and delight . . . he was immoderately given up. But therein he likewise retained such a power and jurisdiction over his very appetite, that he was not so much transported with beauty and outward allurements, as with those advantages of the mind as manifested an extraordinary wit and spirit and knowledge, and administered great pleasure in the conversation.'

It is, of course, impossible to draw any conclusive inference from passages such as these; they merely show that a strong *prima facie* case can be made out in favour of the Pembroke theory. And, indeed, beyond the feeble light thrown by this qualified hypothesis, the whole problem still remains wrapped in the darkness of conjecture. Whether the veil will ever be lifted which now shrouds the mysterious figure of 'Mr W. H.' is a question which Sir Thomas Browne would doubtless have pronounced to be 'above antiquarism'; but we may console ourselves with the thought that, after all, the identity of Shakespeare's friend is a matter of only secondary importance. It is Shakespeare's poetry which is the essential thing. Nor does the right method of interpreting his poetry—in spite of all the inkpots of all the commentators—lie open to any doubt. It is not in elaborate arguments, nor hazardous deductions, nor far-fetched comparisons that the truth about the sonnets is to be found, but in the sonnets themselves. Shakespeare's own words form the best motto for the reader beset with the snares and temptations of a seducing criticism:

> 'No! Let me be obsequious in thy heart;
> And take thou my oblation, poor but free,
> Which is not mix'd with seconds, knows no art,
> But mutual render, only me for thee.'

No one who has read the sonnets in this spirit will ever believe that they are nothing more than literary exercises, or that they were merely written as propitiatory addresses to a patron. These theories belong to the artificialities of criticism, against which Canon Beeching, we are glad to find, makes a decided stand. For to accept them is to ignore what is patent to any reader of the sonnets whose feelings have not been 'mix'd with seconds'—the emotional tone which dominates the entire series.

Thus it has come about that the very poems which Mr Sidney Lee has declared to be devoid of any emotion whatever have been attacked by Hallam for the 'excessive and misplaced affection' which they display. For us it is, perhaps, sufficient to steer a middle course:

> 'O brother, speak with possibilities,
> And do not break into these deep extremes.'

If we cannot recognize anything in Shakespeare's emotion for his friend which is either 'excessive' or 'misplaced', what need is there to be hurried into the opposite extreme, and to deny that the greatest of poets felt any emotion at all?

February 4, 1905

The Pastoral*

In the guide-book of the Muses very little mention is now made of Arcadia. It is briefly referred to as one of those places which only deserve a visit on account of the celebrity which they once enjoyed. The tide of pleasure-seekers has turned aside from it, leaving it high and dry; and one would as soon think of dancing at Vauxhall or of taking lodgings at Pompeii as of wandering, with a sheep-hook and a pipe, over those forgotten lawns. No one now—not even a poet—neglects an imaginary flock to make love to an allegorical shepherdess

> 'By shallow rivers to whose falls
> Melodious birds sing madrigals.'

Nevertheless, Arcady will repay something more than a cursory inspection. Not only have pastoral forms and pastoral images played an important part in the thought and literature of Europe from the days of Theocritus to the days of Marie Antoinette, but some of the greatest masterpieces of language and of art have owed their origin to the pastoral ideal. Yet, though the subject is such a wide one, it has hitherto been hardly touched upon by critics. Mr Walter Greg's study of some of its most interesting phases will therefore be welcomed by every lover of letters. The main subject of his book—the pastoral drama of Elizabethan England—is rich in matter and fertile in

Pastoral Poetry and Pastoral Drama: a Literary Inquiry, with Special Reference to the Pre-Restoration Stage in England, by Walter W. Greg, M.A. London: A. H. Bullen.

suggestion; but he has not limited himself to a consideration of this branch of pastoral alone. His inquiry has been
naturally extended from the drama to English pastoral
poetry in general, and thence, by an easy transition, to
that great body of Italian literature which was the
fountain-head of the pastoral tradition in Europe. Thus
his book contains much more than its title suggests. It is in
reality a collection of studies illustrating, with varying
degrees of detail, the history of the pastoral spirit in Italy
and England, from the earliest times to the Restoration.
Mr Greg has wisely sacrificed unity of design for the
advantages which are afforded by a broad and discursive
method of treatment. He has not been afraid to write at
length of Guarini and Tasso, of Spenser and Sidney, not
merely with reference to the influence which they exercised upon the main stream of pastoral literature, but from
the point of view of their own actual achievements in art.
Mr Greg's criticism is always careful and discriminating;
the chief characteristic of his work is a conscientious
erudition which never sinks into pedantry, and is lightened
by a real humanity and a quiet wit. He is most interesting
when he is most detailed, as in his account of Tasso's
Aminata and his examination of *The Faithful Shepherdess*. His
book is perhaps a little over-burdened by the great number
of outlined plots and condensed poems which it contains;
and though there are many quotations which it is pleasant
to meet, either because one knows them already or because
one does not know them at all, it is somewhat distressing
to have nothing taken for granted. That there is beautiful
poetry in *Comus* is a proposition which hardly needs
demonstration; and who wishes for a paraphrase of
Lycidas? Might not such works as these—after the manner
of less inspired compositions—have been 'taken as read'?

Mr Greg's historical treatment of his subject was
rendered necessary by the very nature of the pastoral,
which was essentially a product of old conventions, an

artificial flower firmly rooted in the past. For us, who can hardly conceive of any art which is not the expression of an individual mind, the point of view of the pastoral writer is peculiarly difficult to understand. His first duty was to be unoriginal; it was only after he had expressed the conventions of his predecessors that he might think of expressing himself. And this explains the disrepute into which the greater number of the most celebrated pastoral works have fallen. Contemporary audiences possessed a clue to their signification which we are without. They saw them set in an atmosphere of traditional beauty; they found in them a whole world of endearing reminiscences and familiar delights. The jilted shepherd, the bewitched shepherdess, the cruel seducer, the faithful lovers—these were not the frigid formulae which we are apt to pronounce them; they were magic symbols evoking long trains of memory and vision and thought, stretching backward and ramifying outward through a hundred pleasant channels, from yesterday's play and last year's romance to the Spanish knights of Montemayor and the lovely ladies of Tasso, to the dreams of Sennazzaro and Petrarch, to Virgil, and to the wooded uplands of Sicily. This was the background —vague and indefinite, but always present—which gave to the particular puppets of Lodge or of Browne or of Randolph their common overmastering charm. We, who have lost apprehension of the background, see the puppets merely as puppets, and wonder how they were ever tolerated. It is only when they are glorified and transformed by the triumphant power of verse—by a Spenser, for instance, or a Milton—that we are really carried off our feet. But even then we are not admiring what our ancestors admired. We do not care whether the *Shepherd's Calendar* owes much or little to the eclogues of Marot; nor can we admit that our appreciation of *Lycidas* was incomplete because we did not know, before it was pointed out to us by Mr Greg, that the poem is in all its parts—

including even the introduction of the Pilot of the Galilean lake—the reflection and the summary of the whole long tradition of pastoral verse.

Undoubtedly the most remarkable instance of a neglected pastoral is the *Arcadia*, one of the books which, as Mr Greg says, 'everybody knows and nobody reads.' The reason both for its vogue and for its neglect is to be found in the same fact—its complete conventionality. The *Arcadia* pleased because it was steeped in the artificial atmosphere through which literature habitually presented itself to the ladies and gentlemen of Elizabeth's Court; and when the literary atmosphere changed it inevitably fell into oblivion. Mr Greg in discussing its prose style passes some severe strictures upon the formal, stilted, and unpliable construction of the Arcadian sentence. 'We cannot but recognize,' he says, 'that in itself Arcadianism was little, if at all, better than Euphuism'; and he goes on to quote, as a specimen of what Sidney *might* have written, the sentence which, if we are to believe Cervantes, excited the enthusiasm of Don Quixote: 'The reason of the unreason which is done to my reason in such manner enfeebles my reason that with reason I lament your beauty.' All this shows clearly enough how strongly even Mr Greg has been impressed by the affectations of the *Arcadia*. But has he been altogether just? At first sight, indeed, there seems very little to choose between Sidney and his predecessors; they are all elaborately contorted together. Yet as one reads on one cannot help feeling a difference. One cannot help feeling that, while Euphues, for instance, is elaborate contortion and little else, there is something real and something beautiful under all the affectations of Sidney. When he writes: 'But with that Dorus blushed, and Pamela smiled, and Dorus the more blushed at her smiling, and she the more smiled at his blushing,' he is, in spite of the obvious pose, saying something which one wants to hear. It is his misfortune to have been buried under the weight of an extinct convention; he is, as it were, lost beneath the complication of his clothes. Euphuism, no one can doubt, is a dead thing rigged out in antiquated raiment; but the *Arcadia* is not dead. Nor is it quite alive; but it is something between the two: it is sleeping. The impression which it leaves upon the mind is strange and elaborate and drowsy; it is like a beautiful dream.

While Mr Greg has failed to appreciate the underlying poetry of the *Arcadia*, he has, on the other hand, exaggerated the dramatic intention of the Elizabethan pastoral plays. He has been so anxious to avoid the common error of dismissing their *dramatis personae* as mere lay figures, devoid of singificance and of art, that he has flown to the opposite extreme, and attributes to them all the characteristics of real human beings. The result is natural enough: he finds the inhabitants of Arcadia not all to his liking. Nearly all the characters in *The Faithful Shepherdess* appear to him to be coarse and immoral, while the lady in *Comus* strikes him as an insufferable prig. These judgments, it is true, are precisely those which one would be inclined to make if one numbered a Cloe among one's acquaintance, or if one happened to come across Milton's lady in real life. But what reason is there for such suppositions? The truth is that Lamb's famous defence of the Restoration comedies applies with far greater force to these pastoral dramas. Their characters are not intended to be representations of reality, so that it is beside the mark to judge them by the standards of the actual world. They belong to a universe which is very different from ours—a universe where there are very few proprieties and no reputations, where the only conventions are the conventions of art, where one can transgress without doing ill, where one can preach without being a bore, where there is nothing to do but to make love, and where everything comes right in the end. To discover in the airy population of Arcadia the weight and the solidity of the material world is to commit a fallacy in perception. And Mr Greg does more than this: he is prepared to mingle the gross creatures of reality with these insubstantial beings; he would weave figures of flesh and blood among the tapestried shapes upon the wall. For this, in effect, is what Mr Greg is doing when he condones Ben Jonson's introduction of realistic rusticity and squalor into the exquisite Arcadian web of his *Sad Shepherd*. 'Jonson,' as Drummond of Hawthornden shrewdly observed, 'bringeth in clowns making mirth and foolish sports, contrary to all other pastorals.' To borrow an analogy from painting, Jonson's introduction of realism has destroyed the harmony of his tones. Mr Greg points to the presence of Audrey in *As You Like It* as a proof of the artistic propriety of a combination of realism with pastoral romance. But the example is fatal to his own contention. For with what consummate skill has Shakespeare softened the roughness and concealed the coarseness of that delightful figure! He has cast an enchantment over it; he has transmuted it for his own purposes; in short, he has brought it into tone with the rest of his picture. We can see the realism of Audrey only through the golden haze of Arcadia. This is what Jonson either would not or could not do. Instead, he tried to achieve the impossible. He tried to put a harlequin by Degas into a *Fête Champêtre* by Watteau. But the result was just what might have been expected: it came on to rain, and there was no fête after all.

July 28, 1906

Bacon as a Man of Letters

THE tercentenary celebration of Bacon's election as Treasurer of Gray's Inn is to be followed by the erection of a statue of the great Lord Chancellor in one of the Inn's open spaces—probably the charming South Square. Nothing could be more fitting than such a memorial in such a spot to one of the most eminent lawyers of England; but it is curious to consider how many other distinguished bodies of men might with equal propriety pay a similar homage to Francis Bacon. Perhaps no man ever lived possessed of such various titles to the admiration of posterity. Besides being a great lawyer, he was a great statesman and a great philosopher, so that his memory deserves honour, not only from the benchers of Gray's Inn, but from Members of Parliament and from the Fellows of the Royal Society. And if none of these claims to distinction had been his—if he had passed his life in private obscurity and had never written a word of his 'Instauratio Magna'—he would still fill a unique place among great Englishmen by virtue of his consummate mastery of the English language. Indeed, such is the strange power of the art of writing that it is through the *Essays* alone that Bacon's fame is today something more than a vague recollection in the minds of his countrymen. He himself would have been the last to be surprised at this. 'As for my Essays,' he says, 'I count them but as the recreations of my other studies, and in that sort purpose to continue them; though I am not ignorant that those kind of writings would, with less pains and embracement, perhaps, yield more lustre and reputation to my name than those others which I have in hand.' Bacon belongs to the very small band of our prose writers of whom it can be said with certainty that their popularity is as great as their achievement. Other writers of equal merit—Sir Thomas Browne, for instance, and Gibbon, and Burke—though they are widely read, are not read universally; none of their works is popular in the sense in which *The Pilgrim's Progress* is popular, and *Gulliver's Travels*, and *The Essays or Counsels, Civil and Moral*. And Bacon, no less than Bunyan and Swift, is read primarily for his matter. 'The King,' he says of Henry VII, 'to speak of him in terms equal to his deserving, was one of the best sort of wonders: a wonder for wise men'; and the words apply with singular exactness to the author of the *Essays*. Everyone must feel, after a reading in that fascinating book, that there indeed is 'a wonder for wise men', that there is the very soul of wisdom, the very embodiment of clear, profound, and powerful thought. 'Some books are to be tasted, others to be swallowed, and some few to be chewed and digested.' Who can doubt into which of these classes the *Essays* fall? Let us take a single example of their concentration of meaning. In the essay on 'Simulation and Dissimulation' Bacon discusses with wonderful subtlety and judgment the various shades of concealment and deceit, the precise circumstances in which [in his opinion] they are permissible, and the rules which [he holds] should guide a good man in his use of them. He concludes in a sentence which sums up within itself his view of the whole philosophy of the subject: 'The best composition and temperature is, to have openness in fame and opinion; secrecy in habit; dissimulation in seasonable use; and a power to feign if there be no remedy.' [We may not like his conclusion—for ourselves, we repudiate it as immoral and ignoble—but who can deny that it is an epitome of the worldly wisdom on the matter under consideration?]

Yet, in spite of the amazing force and weight of Bacon's

matter, it is clear that the fascination of his work depends no less upon his style. If it is true that the generality of readers explore him for the sake of what he has to tell them, it is equally certain that they would never have troubled to find that out if he had not taken care to tell it them with exquisite art. To the lover of fine prose his writing brings a pleasure which no other English master quite succeeds in producing, and which, in its precise flavour, is called up by only one or two other writers in the literature of the world. In some ways the temper of his art is rather French than English. He is a supreme master of the sententious style—a style which has been practised by only one other English writer of the first rank, Burke, and by him only, as it were, incidentally, while in France the greatest writers have made it their own. Certainly the best of his aphorisms are worthy to take rank beside the most brilliant of La Rochefoucauld's and the most beautiful of La Bruyère's. How many of them one can recall with joy! 'Revenge is a kind of wild justice'; 'He that hath wife and children hath given hostages to fortune'; 'We take cunning for a sinister or crooked wisdom'; 'Men fear death as children fear to go in the dark'; 'There is no excellent beauty that hath not some strangeness in the proportion.' But it is easier to begin making such quotations than to stop. Yet we must remember that there is this important difference between the epigrams of Bacon and those of his French rivals—his form part of a related whole, while the others are detached jewels separately set. Thus the true charm of Bacon's writing cannot be revealed in single sentences; it lies in the elaboration, the interconnexion, the orderly development, the gradual exposition of a series of subtle and splendid thoughts. Of modern writers, Montesquieu, perhaps, comes nearest to him, but Montesquieu lacks the rich colouring which distinguishes Bacon's style. It is this characteristic—this combination of colour and of thought

—which gives Bacon his unique position among prose writers. The great colourists—witness Sir Thomas Browne —have as a rule no very definite thoughts to show us, only gorgeous imaginations; while, on the other hand, the great thinkers—Swift, for instance—content themselves with clarity and vigour of expression. We must go back to the ancients—to some of the glowing pages of Thucydides or the sombre meditations of Tacitus—to find a parallel with what is finest in the prose of Bacon. As Taine admirably says, 'ce qui distingue celui-ci des autres, c'est que chez lui l'image ne fait que concentrer la méditation.' A famous passage from the first of the essays—'Of Truth' —affords an example of this rare concatenation of qualities:

'This same truth is a naked and open daylight, that doth not show the masques, and mummeries, and triumphs of the world, half so stately and daintily as candle-lights. Truth may perhaps come to the price of a pearl, that showeth best by day; but it will not rise to the price of a diamond or carbuncle that showeth best in varied lights. A mixture of a lie doth ever add pleasure. Doth any man doubt that if there were taken out of men's minds vain opinions, flattering hopes, false valuations, imaginations as one would, and the like, but it would leave the minds of a number of men poor shrunken things, full of melancholy and indisposition, and unpleasing to themselves?'

There is a happy valiancy in many of Bacon's phrases, which, while they betray the lover of words, yet never show a trace of mannerism of affectation. Thus his style is always unmistakable. Who but Bacon, for instance, could have written sentences at once as sober and as racy as these?—'Suspicions that the mind of itself gathers are but buzzes; but suspicions that are artificially nourished, and put into men's heads by the tales and whisperings of others, have stings.' And—'Beauty is as summer fruits, which are easy to corrupt and cannot last; and, for the most part, it makes a dissolute youth and an age a little out of countenance.' Who but Bacon would have described the flattering of counsellors as 'a song of *Placebo*'? Who but he could have invented that memorable maxim, so splendid and so bold in its concentration: 'To be master of the sea is an abridgment of monarchy'?

Bacon was, in the best sense of the expression, a man of the world. There can be no doubt that he was sincere in his religion, and that he was a genuine lover of the arts. But these things were not fundamental to him. He was not essentially spiritual like Pascal, nor essentially an artist like Keats. His philosophy was utilitarian, and his deepest interests were fixed upon the workings and the welfare of human society. His style reflects his character. It has no poetical mystery, no power of vague suggestion and romance. It never reaches the heights, nor explores the depths; but it is strong, subtle, clear, and it glows with an intellectual beauty. It comes nearest to passion when it touches upon the two greatest of worldly goods—virtue and truth. 'This is the strength and blood to virtue, to contemn things that be desired, and to neglect that which is feared.' That is a sublime sentence; and this is another: 'Certainly it is heaven upon earth to have a man's mind move in charity, rest in providence, and turn upon the poles of truth.' And when in the *New Atlantis* Bacon describes the journeys of the Fellows of Solomon's House, his writing becomes invested with an unwonted eloquence. ' "But thus you see we maintain a trade, not for gold, silver, or jewels; nor for silks; nor for spices; nor any other commodity of matter; but only for God's first creature, which was light: to have light, I say, of the growth of all the world." And when he had said this, he was silent; and so were we all.' It is difficult to remember that he who wrote thus could turn his mind without an effort to the exposition of the most effective arrangements for gardens, the best means of frustrating curiosity, or the surest methods of obtaining despatch in business; but Bacon's mind was universal in its comprehensiveness; there was nothing in the world of which he could not write. And this must be his praise—that while other men have shown us the spirit of an age in their writings, or the spirit of a cause or a belief, or the spirit of their own dreams and their own desires, Bacon has compressed into his immortal pages nothing more nor less than the spirit of the world itself.

October 24, 1908

The Poetry of John Donne*

THE history of the poetical reputation of John Donne is one of the most curious in literature. During his lifetime, his poems, with very few exceptions, were unpublished; but they were widely circulated in manuscript, and became the object of a universal and unbounded admiration. Certainly in the eyes of the great majority of his contemporaries Donne was by far the most eminent writer of his age—which was the age of Bacon and Shakespeare. The first edition of his poems appeared in 1633, two years after his death, and was followed by half a dozen more in the course of the next thirty years. During that period his fame was at its height. Carey, in the well-known lines of his *Elegy*, expressed the opinion of the day:

> 'Here lies a King that ruled as he thought fit
> The universal monarchy of wit.'

His manner of writing was as much imitated by the poetasters of the time as that of Pope in the eighteenth century or that of Tennyson in the nineteenth. The reaction began with Dryden, who ventured to make what was then the daring statement that Donne was 'the greatest wit, though not the greatest poet, of our nation.' For the next two hundred years he remained in almost absolute neglect. In the eighteenth century Pope paid him the very doubtful compliment of 'versifying' his Satires, and Dr Johnson, in his *Life of Cowley*, delivered what he no

* *The Poems of John Donne*. Edited from the old Editions and numerous Manuscripts, with Introductions and Commentary, by Herbert J. C. Grierson, M.A. 2 vols. Oxford: At the Clarendon Press.

doubt believed was the *coup de grâce* to the whole school of writers of which Donne was the chief. With the coming of the romantics, his reputation slightly rose; Coleridge and De Quincey admired him, but they did not popularize him. During the Victorian epoch he was regarded in general as a mere curiosity, and it was not until the appearance of Mr Grosart's edition in 1872 that it was possible to become acquainted with his work save in the rare and obscure little volumes of the seventeenth century. In 1896 the admirable edition of Mr Chambers in the Muses' Library for the first time brought Donne within the reach of the average reader, and for the last fifteen years there has probably been more genuine interest taken in his poetry by lovers of English literature than during the whole preceding period since the days of Dryden. The full and scholarly edition which Professor Grierson has just published is at once a proof of this growing interest in Donne's work and an assurance of its increase in the future. In two ways his edition is peculiarly valuable. By the judicious collection of numerous illustrative passages, particularly from the early Fathers and from Donne's own sermons, Professor Grierson has been able to throw much new light on the intricate meanings of the text. His work on the text itself—involving the difficult and arduous task of a thorough collation not only of the early editions but of a great number of the contemporary manuscripts—is even more important. His purely critical and literary observations, though always of interest, seem hardly to be of sufficient weight to justify their inclusion with the rest of his work. The edition would certainly have gained if its scope had been limited to the establishment and exposition of an authoritative text of Donne's poetry. It would then, in all probability, have been final. As it is, an element of mortality has crept in with Professor Grierson's personal—and, therefore, perishable—appreciations of his author.

Donne's work is peculiarly interesting, not only on account of its high intrinsic merits, but owing to the extraordinary strength and the no less extraordinary diversity of its influence upon subsequent writers. It is a curious paradox that a poet whose traces are to be found all over English literature should still be almost unknown to the majority of English readers. It would be difficult, for instance, to name two works more remote from each other in style, in subject, in feeling, in general conception, than Butler's *Hudibras* and Crashaw's *Hymn to Saint Teresa*; yet both the ingenious ribaldry of the one and the mystical frenzies of the other are the direct offspring of Donne's poetry. More important, because more far-reaching, was his influence on Dryden. Dryden, we know, was in his youth an enthusiastic disciple of Donne, and his early work shows the signs of his admiration plainly enough. There is nothing surprising in this. Apart from Chaucer, Donne was the first English writer to grasp to the full the importance of the realistic and intellectual elements in poetry. It was he who, by leading a revolt against the sugared and sensuous style of Spenser, opened the way to that great movement in our literature which culminated in the *Satires* of Pope. And it was through Dryden that the way lay. Dryden's eminently rationalistic and mundane mind recognized in Donne the master who could teach him how to use verse both as an instrument of argumentative exposition and as a brilliant mirror of actual life. Having learnt this, he went a step further, discarded what was *baroque* and unessential in Donne's manner, and introduced once for all the modern spirit into poetry. Thus, in a sense, he superseded Donne, but the magnificent original conception of the great Elizabethan lies at the root of Dryden's finest work, and of that of his numerous spiritual progeny. Just as *Endymion* is implicit in the *Faerie Queen*, so is *English Bards and Scotch Reviewers* implicit in the *Satires* of Donne.

But though the main importance of Donne's influence lay in this direction, the actual characteristics of his poetry itself are curiously complex, and the essential nature of his work differs entirely from that of any of his successors. The intellectuality of Dryden and Pope, the mysticism of Crashaw and Vaughan, the gallantry of Cowley, the bitter wit of Butler, all these elements are to be found in him, not side by side, but completely interfused and compounded together into a strange and unique whole. It is here that the peculiar interest of his poetry lies—in the amazing many-sidedness of the personality which it reveals. It shows us a man who was at once religious, sensual, erudite, passionate, and argumentative. 'He combined,' says De Quincey, 'what no other man has ever done—the last sublimation of dialectical subtlety and address with the most impassioned majesty.' His love poems are probably the most extraordinary in the world. Loaded with complicated reasonings, learned allusions to obscure writers, abstruse references to philosophical systems, it seems almost impossible that they should be anything but frigid and absurd. And, of course, many critics—with Dr Johnson at the head of them—have failed to see more in Donne's poetry than a preposterous collection of 'conceits'. Dryden himself, with the blindness of a reformer, wrote of Donne that 'he affects the metaphysics, not only in his satires, but in his amorous verses, where nature only should reign; and perplexes the minds of the fair sex with nice speculations of philosophy when he should engage their hearts, and entertain them with the softnesses of love.' The criticism seems perfectly just until we turn to the poems themselves, and find that Donne really has achieved the impossible. The ardours of his passionate soul transfuse his antiquated mannerisms, his contorted and remote conceptions, and fill them with an intensely human significance. He has the art of endowing the strangest speculations with a personal thrill:

> 'I long to talk with some old lover's ghost,
> Who died before the god of Love was born.'

He can make a far-fetched, complicated simile the occasion for a lyrical outburst of astonishing beauty:

> 'O more than moon!
> Draw not up tears to drown me in thy sphere,
> Weep me not dead in thine arms. . . .'

Or he can turn an epigram into an intimate confession of adoration:

> 'I must confess, it could not choose but be
> Profane, to think thee anything but thee.'

Nor is it only in his love poems that the remarkable qualities of Donne's poignant and powerful nature are apparent. In his elegies, his satires, and his devotional verses the same bizarre and highly-strung individuality makes itself felt. Perhaps the most characteristic of all his works are the two 'Anniversaries' written to commemorate the early death at the age of fifteen of Elizabeth Drury, the daughter of one of Donne's patrons. In these strange poems his genius seems to pour itself forth without restraint in a sort of intoxication. No one has a right to consider himself a true worshipper of Donne unless he can admire wholeheartedly these extraordinary productions. Whether Professor Grierson comes within the category is a little doubtful. He seems to apologize for the tremendous and elaborate structure of hyperboles which Donne has erected over the grave of this young girl. But here apologies are out of place; one must either reject wholly or accept wholly; Donne is either revolting or magnificent. Probably it is the very intensity of his seriousness that tends to mislead some of his modern readers. To him God and Heaven were blazing and palpitating realities, and the human soul was a miracle about which no exaggeration of statement was possible. He saw in Elizabeth Drury, not only the type, but the actual presence, of all that is most marvellous in the spirit of man.

> 'One, whose clear body was so pure and thin,
> Because it need disguise no thought within:
> 'Twas but a through-light scarf, her mind t' inroll;
> Or exhalation breathed out from her Soul.'

And he meant not less, but more, than what he wrote of her:

> 'She to whose person Paradise adhered
> As courts to Princes, she whose eyes ensphered
> Starlight enough to have made the South control
> (Had she been there) the star-full Northern Pole,
> She, she is gone; she is gone; when thou knowest this,
> What fragment rubbidge this world is
> Thou knowest, and that it is not worth a thought.'

In such lines as these one recognizes the same spirit which led Donne, on his death-bed, to wrap himself in his shroud to have his portrait painted. For that strange nature rhetorical eccentricity seems to have been the sincerest expression of mystical ravishment, just as dialectical quibbling was the natural language of his most passionate love.

January 18, 1913

C. The Seventeenth Century

Forgotten Poets *

OUR modern literary pantheon is large enough to include
every variety of divinity; and the series of reprints which
Professor Saintsbury is now editing shows that the minor
deities no less than the Olympians come in for their share
of incense. It may, indeed, be questioned whether Professor Saintsbury has not pushed the cult for the fugitive
and the obscure a little too far. He has let down his drag-
net into the ocean of Caroline poetry, and has fished out a
handful of small fry which would have slipped through the
meshes of any ordinary criticism. It is only, however, in
one sense that the fry are small. The four poets whose
works are reprinted in the present volume take up between
them over eight hundred large octavo pages, most of
which are double-columned. Surely the resuscitation of
such a vast quantity of matter was a serious responsibility;
and is it possible altogether to admit that the act was
justifiable, when we remember that there is not a single
line in the whole mass of the collection which rises above
the second-rate?

But such doubts—though we cannot but feel them—are
perhaps a little ungracious, for the volume possesses so
many points of interest that it is easy to forget the porten-
tous mediocrity which is really its dominant feature.
Professor Saintsbury in his introductory notices has laid
special stress upon the light which his poets throw upon
the development of English versification; and it is true that
this important, though somewhat technical, subject can be

---

* *Minor Poets of the Caroline Period.* Edited by George Saintsbury,
M.A. Vol. I. Oxford: at the Clarendon Press.

amply illustrated by their works. But why does Professor Saintsbury stop there? The truth is that it is not only the versification of the period, but the whole tendency of Elizabethan poetry, which is epitomized in this volume. The poems are poor poems; they belong to the fag-end of a great tradition; they exaggerate its weaknesses and minimize its strength. But their very faults help us to understand more clearly the true nature of the great age which was theirs. The splendours of triumphant art are often so dazzling as to blind us to the actual detail of its qualities; and it is only when we have coolly examined a bad imitation that we come to comprehend the hidden values of the original.

The poems of Patrick Hannay afford an excellent example of the orthodox Elizabethan tradition. Their fancy, their naïveté, their easy grace, make them constantly delightful; they are composed of a series of pretty details set in a background of delicate, if conventional, romance. The poet, walking 'in the shade which top-entwining trees had made', listens to the music of the birds in the branches:

'Ravished with liking of their songs,
    I thought I understood
The several language to each 'longs,
    That lodges in that wood.
        Most *Philomel*
        Did me compel
    To listen to her song,
        In sugar'd strains,
        While she complains
    Of Tyrant Tereus' wrong.'

The rest of the poem consists of the story of Philomel, which the bird proceeds to give utterance to for the next hundred stanzas. Hannay's description of the nightingale's song may aptly be applied to his own poetry: it is 'sugar'd.' That is at once its merit and its fault; for Hannay's sweetness is unrelieved by any other quality. Hi.

form is always careless and his thought is always common-place. His narratives meander through a wilderness of unruly ornament and tangled verse: and only stop to remind us at irregular intervals that honesty is the best policy, that in this world nothing is permanent, and that good children obey their parents. Nor does Hannay in his most sugary moments ever produce a really first-rate piece of confectionery. His sweetness is of the kind which easily cloys, and it would be as difficult to read through *Sheretine and Mariana* at a single sitting as to eat the whole of the icing on a wedding-cake.

The *Pharonnida* of William Chamberlayne presents precisely similar characteristics, but in an exaggerated degree. If Hannay's verse resembles a shrubbery thick with brambles which delay the traveller at every step, *Pharonnida* is a tropical forest where the luxuriance of festoons and undergrowth must be hewn through by sheer force. That extraordinary poem, with its vast intrigue in the recesses of which the author, no less than the reader, loses his way, is in reality no more than the framework for an endless succession of descriptive details. In these details lies the whole value of the poem, and at their best they give Chamberlayne a place only just below the great and unmistakable poets of our language. Such lines as

> 'Heart-cheering chrysolytes,
> With rubies set, which to adorn them twist
> Embraces with the temperate amethyst,'

show a command of language not unworthy of a spiritual ancestor of Keats. But Chamberlayne falls below mediocrity more often than he rises above it, and his incredible prolixity still further emphasizes the flatness of the common level of his verse. Quotation from him is rendered peculiarly difficult by this very fact, for it is only possible to obtain the full impression of his easy, diffuse, and infinitely decorated style by reading through several pages.

The following passage, however, though necessarily abridged, will give some idea of the run of an ordinary sentence—or, rather, clause—in *Pharonnida*:

> '. . . A purling stream; whose spring did live,
> When from the hill's cool womb broke forth, within
> A grotto; whence before it did begin
> To take its weeping farewell, into all
> The various forms restrictive Art could call
> Her elemental instruments into
> Obedience by, it courts the admiring view
> Of pleased spectators—here, exalted by
> Clear aqueducts, in showers it from those high
> Supporters falls; now turned into a thin
> Vapour, in that heaven's painted bow is seen;
> Now it supplies the place of air, and to
> A choir of birds gives breath, which all seemed flew
> From thence for fear, when the same element,
> With such a voice as seas imprisoned rent
> Including rocks, doth roar . . . so, Proteus-like,
> Returned from what did fear or wonder strike,
> The liquid nymph, resuming her own shape
> Within a marble square, a clear escape,
> Till from her winding stream the river takes
> Still fresh supplies, from that fair fountain makes.'

These lines, published as late as 1659, yet belong clearly enough to the main school of Elizabethan poetry—the school of Spenser. The absence of concision, the lack of distinguished thought, the intricacy of detail, so obvious in Chamberlayne are no less patent in the *Faerie Queene*. But we shall search in vain in the later poet for the unending glamour and the compelling charm of his great predecessor. Chamberlayne seems to possess in double measure all the unessential qualities of Spenser, and to lack the only essential one—his inspiration. He is a Spenser run to seed. He resembles in his winding elaboration the 'purling stream' of his own poem, which, though the water is the same, has wandered very far indeed from the fountain-head.

The other two poets in Professor Saintsbury's collection —Edward Benlowes and Katherine Phillips—are representatives of a precisely contrary tradition, that which had its origin in the amazing genius of Donne. This is, indeed, their only point of resemblance, for they differ from one another no less than they differ from Chamberlayne or Hannay. Like their master, the great Dean of St Paul's, they have entered into revolt against the Spenserian method; and in their reaction from the orthodox style, with its diffuseness, its conventional insipidity, and its easy sweetness, they have flown into the opposite extreme. They are so compact as to run the risk of obscurity; their imagery is drawn, not from a fancied world of fable and romance, but from the everyday occurrences of real life; and their hatred of the commonplace makes them load their poetry with an accumulation of complicated, extraordinary, and often grotesque thoughts. These peculiarities are to be found in every page of *Theophila*, Benlowes's enormous poem on the soul. He seems determined never to say the expected thing. He is willing to be rugged, obscure, ridiculous, so long as he is always original. At the creation of the world Nature was a callow bird whose sprouting feathers were effects springing from the universal cause. The carbuncles on drunkards' noses are link-boys lighting them through the night. Warning his readers to repent before they are overtaken by old age, he says:

> 'Ere in thy pocket thou thine eyes dost wear;
> Ere thy bones serve for calender;
> Ere in thy hand's thy leg, or silver in thy hair;
> Preventing physic use.'

This is Benbowes's way of talking of a walking-stick and a pair of spectacles.

The poems of Katherine Philips—'the matchless Orinda', as she was called in her own day—are somewhat tame in comparison with the extravagances of *Theophila*. While Benlowes found his inspiration in Donne's religious poems, Mrs Phillips found hers in his secular verse, and her lyrics resemble those of Cowley, though they lack the intellectual adroitness and the depth of feeling of the author of 'The Mistress' and the elegy on Harvey. They are nevertheless nearly always graceful and never ordinary; so that, if one can forget how far they have been surpassed in their own manner, they make pleasant reading. For instance, her comparison between two friends and a pair of compasses, which 'are, and yet they are not, two', is ingeniously worked out:

> 'Each follows where the other leans,
> And what each does this other means.
> And as when one foot does stand fast,
> And t'other circles seeks to cast,
> The steady part does regulate
> And make the wanderer's motion straight;
> So friends are only two in this,
> T' reclaim each other when they miss.'

It is only when they have been compared with Donne's well-known verses on the same subject that these lines seem to lose their point. Mrs Phillips, like the other poets of Professor Saintsbury's volume, represented a moribund tradition. The style of Donne was already giving place to the style of Dryden, just as the genius of Milton was beginning to triumph in the domain over which Spenser's spirit had ruled so long and gloriously. The *rois fainéants* of the old dynasty were destined to fall before these vigorous usurpers. Professor Saintsbury's volume contains the last echo of Elizabethan poetry, before it was silenced for ever by the classicism of the eighteenth century; and across the gulf which separates them from us the songs of Chamber-

layne and of Benlowes, of Hannay and of Katherine
Philips, sound strangely and dimly in our ears:

> 'Only a sense
> Remains of them, like the omnipotence
> Of music, when the inspired voice and lute
> Languish, ere yet the responses are mute.'

January 27, 1906

Milton

THE tercentenary of the year of Milton's birth, which is being celebrated at Cambridge by an Exhibition of portraits and manuscripts, to be followed later by a performance of *Comus*, suggests, after the manner of anniversaries, some questionings as to the value of Milton's achievement and his place in the history of letters. That his place is a very high one no lover of poetry today would wish to dispute, for never has Milton's fame been more assured or more widely recognized than at the present moment. But if the quantity of his merit can admit of no doubt whatever, its quality is not quite so easy to decide upon. In more ways than one Milton's genius presents difficulties and contradictions to the critic who attempts to sum up in a single judgment the nature of his work as a whole. To the world at large he stands out as before all things the poet of sublimity, of austere and awful grandeur, walking in a noble severity among the highest places of art. But if we open his pages, we are struck by a very different impression; we are overwhelmed by a flowing river of enchanting sound, by a mass of words which seem to be there for no other reason than because they are beautiful, and we begin to feel that the real fascination of poetry such as this is simply the fascination of rhetoric. Traditionally, Milton is the greatest of religious poets, and that fundamentally the temper of his mind was profoundly religious it is impossible to doubt. Yet the part of his work which has least withstood the assaults of time—which is most obviously and certainly out of date at the present day —is his theology, while his highest claim to immortality rests upon the amazing splendour and the imperishable glamour with which he has invested the ministers of vice. It is, however, easy to perceive one common element in all these conflicting qualities—one characteristic which, from the beginning to the end of his poetic career, never deserted Milton—his noble and passionate love of art. He is the supreme artist of our race; that, surely, must be the first and last word in any appreciation of the author of *Paradise Lost*. And it is precisely from this point of view that Milton may be most clearly contrasted with the only figure in English literature which, without a shadow of a doubt, towers above his own. Shakespeare was not primarily an artist, in the sense in which the word may be applied to Milton—the sense which connotes a method no less than a result. He worked as no conscientious artist would work, hastily and unevenly; he produced a *King Lear* one day, a *Timon of Athens* the next; he was 'fancy's child'. No doubt his method was that best adapted to his temperament, and it would be rash indeed to affirm that any other method could have produced a greater body of achievement; but it was not the method of the artist. Who can imagine Milton even dreaming of writing the kind of stuff that it pleased Shakespeare to throw off in some of his careless hours? But the comparison becomes still more clearly marked if for Shakespeare we substitute one of the average poets of Milton's youth. What a difference there is between the exquisite unforced lyrics of the Elizabethans and the consummate songs of *Comus*! It is the difference between a wild rose and a rose in a garden bed. Sir Henry Wotton, who was an acute critic, noticed the change at once. He was 'ravished', he wrote to Milton, by 'a certain Dorique delicacy in your Songs and Odes, wherunto I must plainly confess to have seen yet nothing parallel in our Language.' The publication of *Comus* did indeed mark an epoch in English literature; henceforward our poetry could never be the half-unconscious thing that it had been before. In

Milton's hands it became an elaborate product, the out-come of patient care and infinite craft. The ideal poem was 'not to be raised from the heat of youth, or the vapours of wine, like that which flows at waste from the pen of some vulgar amorist, or the trencher fury of a rhyming parasite, nor to be obtained by the invocation of Dame Memory and her Siren daughters, but by devout prayer to that eternal Spirit who can enrich with all utterance and knowledge, and sends out his Seraphim with the hallowed fire of his altar to touch and purify the lips of whom he pleases; to this must be added industrious and select reading, steady observation, insight into all seemly and generous arts and affairs.' Such was the spirit which went to the making of *Paradise Lost*.

It is the artist that appears most distinctly in what is perhaps the most sympathetic of the many portraits now gathered together at the Memorial Exhibition at Christ's College—the charming presentment of Milton as a young man, which usually hangs in the College Hall, and a reproduction of which is to be found in the interesting catalogue of the collection ('Milton Tercentenary: the Portraits, Prints, and Writings of John Milton, Exhibited at Christ's College, 1908'). The authenticity of the picture is merely traditional; but it is impossible to believe that the beautiful oval face with the great eyes and the arched nose and the long hair could have belonged to any save a poet, or to any poet save John Milton. There is a curious deli-cacy, an aristocratic refinement, about these fascinating features which inevitably put one in mind of Milton's own account of that 'certain niceness of nature, an honest haughtiness and self-esteem either of what I was or what I might be,' which, he says, kept him above the 'low descents of mind' when he was a young man. The expression of the countenance is full of the exclusiveness and of the preciosity of a youthful artist who has just begun to recognize his own high worth; but there is more in it than that. There is a dreamy sensuousness in the eyes and in the full lips which betrays the author of the lovely and delicious cadences of 'L'Allegro' and the 'Arcades' and 'Lycidas'. That, in spite of his Puritanism, there was a strain in Milton of what might almost be called paganism, no reader of his works can doubt. His well-known observation upon the chief attributes of poetry—that it is simple, sensuous, and passionate—is in itself an indication of this, and his poems show clearly enough that the definition was by no means a random one. The truth is, it would be difficult to name a poet who was more completely occupied with the 'sensuous' side of things—the side, that is to say, which appeals directly to the senses. He has none of the intellectual subtlety of Donne, none of the psychological intensity of Pope, none of the spiritual tenderness of Wordsworth; his merits depend almost entirely upon a faculty of lofty and grandiose vision coupled with a complete mastery of the resources of verbal sound. His imagination, within its own province, was supreme; but it was, so to speak, a material imagination, perpetually concerned with objects which, however vast and however splendid, still remained objects of sense. Between his imagination and that of Shakespeare, with its lightning flashes into the heart of man and the mystery of the universe, what a gulf is fixed! Perhaps the most remarkable fact about Milton's genius is that he never allowed his 'sensuousness' to get the better of his art. It is certain that he realized the danger, for, alike in his earliest work and in his latest, in *Comus* as in *Samson*, there are traces of an inward struggle, of an effort to shake off the thraldom of physical beauty, of a determination to worship only the highest and best. 'Yet beauty, though injurious, hath strange power,' exclaim the Chorus in *Samson* after the departure of Dalila, and the phrase might be taken as a summary of the curious conflict of ideals which finds its synthesis in Milton's art.

Underlying and supporting his artistic consciousness there was, of course, that force of character which makes Milton so striking and eminent a figure in the history, not only of literature, but of the world. The high determination with which at the beginning of his career he set out to accomplish a task of superhuman difficulty, and the triumphant success which crowned the guiding resolution of his life—these are things for which it is difficult to find a parallel, and which, when one reflects upon them, seem more thrilling than the strangest romance. Yet the moral qualities that enabled him to achieve so much brought with them another characteristic of a less pleasant nature —a characteristic which is the chief cause of the often-expressed dislike of Milton as a man—his lack of humour. If he had taken himself less seriously, perhaps he would never have written *Paradise Lost*; and the author of *Paradise Lost* no doubt had a right to take himself seriously; but who can help regretting that he took himself as seriously as he did? One wonders what Shakespeare would have said to some of the autobiographical references in Milton's prose works. But it is uncharitable to raise comparisons. We must, after all, take great men as we find them. If Milton was a confirmed egotist, he was none the less the creator of Satan; and even his egotism, if we are to believe Coleridge, was not without its value. 'It is a sense of his intense egotism,' says that fine critic, 'that gives me the greatest pleasure in reading Milton's works. The egotism of such a man is a revelation of spirit.'

July 4, 1908

French Poetry*

'THE common neglect of French poetry by English lovers of literature' affords the text for a series of interesting and sympathetic studies by Mr John Bailey on the work of some of the great poets of France. It has been Mr Bailey's object to combat 'the widespread opinion that French poetry is merely rhetoric in verse', and to prove 'how much pleasure may be got out of the French poets even by those whose conception of poetry makes them demand of it things far above rhetoric.' It is perhaps a little doubtful whether the neglect of which Mr Bailey complains is quite so general as he seems to suppose; but there can be no doubt at all that his essays will go far to dispel any delusions which may still be lingering in the minds of his readers as to the true value of the poetic achievement of our neighbours. By a happy chance the publication of Mr Bailey's volume synchronizes with that of Mr St John Lucas's excellent anthology of French verse, which forms an ideal companion to Mr Bailey's essays—an appendix, as it were, of *pièces justificatives*. The underlying spirit of both books is the same. Both are concerned almost entirely with the poetry of the Renaissance and the nineteenth century; neither extends any very warm appreciation to the poetical productions of the eighteenth century or of the *grand siècle* of Louis XIV. So far as Mr Lucas's volume is concerned, this can hardly be

* (1) *The Claims of French Poetry: Nine Studies in the Greater French Poets* by John C. Bailey. London: A. Constable & Co. (2) *The Oxford Book of French Verse: Thirteenth Century—Nineteenth Century*. Chosen by St John Lucas. Oxford: at the Clarendon Press.

wondered at; for his plan of selection excludes narrative and dramatic verse, and even the most ardent supporter of the classical school must admit that the lyric was not a plant that flourished in France from the days of Malherbe to the coming of the Romantics. Mr Lucas, however, is surely a little unfair in his treatment of Malherbe, to whom he imputes a 'mechanical accuracy' and a 'frigid intelligence', quoting with approval Banville's amusing commentary on Boileau's famous phrase, 'enfin Malherbe vint'—upon which, the Romantic poet adds,

> 'la Poésie,
> En le voyant arriver, s'en alla.'

It is always easy to deny poetic inspiration to a writer whose most striking qualities are those of refinement, proportion, and clarity; how often, for instance, has the charge of 'cold correctness' been raised against that master of moving beauty and concentrated passion—Alexander Pope. In the case of Malherbe the accusation is refuted by Mr Lucas's own volume, which contains, of course, the poignant sonnet, 'Sur la Mort de son Fils', and the noble and lovely 'Consolation à M. du Périer'.

> 'Mais elle était du monde, où les plus belles choses
>   Ont le pire destin;
> Et rose elle a vécu ce que vivent les roses,
>   L'espace d'un matin,'—

Who can fail to perceive, in the flawless perfection of such lines as these, something more than 'mechanical accuracy' and 'frigid intelligence'?

Mr Bailey, though he says nothing of Malherbe, is as hostile as Mr Lucas to the whole school of classical poetry of which Malherbe was the forerunner and the prophet. This is all the more to be regretted, since his essays show clearly enough that Mr Bailey possesses in no small degree that quality of sympathy without which all criticism is a

vain and empty thing. A good critic is like a good talker—
he must know the difficult art of 'bringing out' an author,
of realizing his strong points, of making him show himself
at his very best; and this is precisely what Mr Bailey
achieves in his delightful studies of Marot and Ronsard,
André Chénier and Victor Hugo, Hérédia and Leconte de
Lisle. Sometimes, in fact, he errs, if he errs at all, through
an excess of appreciation. His treatment of Victor Hugo,
for instance, is lacking in certainty owing to his desire to
pass over the great Frenchman's shortcomings as lightly as
possible. It is not that Mr Bailey fails to recognize what
these faults are. He animadverts more than once upon
Hugo's egotism and bombast, his love of shoddy antitheses
and journalistic cant; but he does not attempt to decide
how far these qualities are essential to Hugo's whole spirit,
or whether they are merely superficial; he is content to
notice them, and to pass them by. The final criticism of
Hugo—that which will discriminate accurately and com-
prehensively between his grain and his chaff—has yet to
be written. In the meantime let us be thankful for
Mr Bailey's wholehearted appreciation of his grain.

The only seventeenth-century poet who finds a welcome
in Mr Bailey's volume is La Fontaine; and it says much
for his study of the charming fabulist that it may be read
with pleasure and profit, even after the brilliant essay by
Sainte-Beuve on the same subject. Mr Bailey, however,
selects La Fontaine, not as representative of his age, but
as exceptional in it; he hails his work with a sigh of relief
as a comfortable little oasis amid the vast desert of
classicism. This is characteristic of Mr Bailey's general
attitude towards French poetical literature, which he
regards as deserving of admiration solely on account of the
achievements of the early Renaissance writers, and of the
great Romantics of the nineteenth century. Indeed, the
explicit purpose of his book is to press the claims of French
poetry upon English readers from this point of view.

French critics themselves, he admits, have always regarded the work of Racine as the most valuable contribution which their nation has made to the literature of the world; but his contention is that the French critics are wrong, that, in effect, Racine deserves very little attention, and that a true understanding of French poetry will only be reached by those who rivet their regard upon those manifestations of it which are most directly opposed to the influence of Racine's school. On the face of it, this line of argument seems a little paradoxical. What would Mr Bailey himself say if a French writer were to assure him that the only valuable elements in English literature were those which owed their origin to Dryden and Pope, while it was safe to neglect all the most characteristic works of the Elizabethan age? Would he not reply that to disregard the Elizabethans was to disregard what lay at the very heart of the national genius? And is not this precisely the reply which, *mutatis mutandis*, a French critic would make to Mr Bailey's attack on Racine and the *grand siècle*? There can surely be no doubt at all that Racine represents what is most French in French poetry, just as Shakespeare represents what is most English in English poetry, although, of course, it may still be open to question whether what is most French and what is most poetical coincide. Mr Bailey argues at some length to show that Racine is not poetical at all in the highest sense of the term; but—to adapt Burke's famous phrase—it is a dangerous thing to indict the ideals of a whole nation, and Mr Bailey's arguments, though they are always interesting, do not carry conviction. After determining by a process of analysis what the qualities are which go to constitute great poetry, he asks the question: 'Does Racine possess these qualities?' and, on discovering that he does not, draws the conclusion that he cannot be a great poet. But would it not be safer to conclude that Mr Bailey's analysis of the elements of great poetry is incomplete? And, indeed, the

more closely one looks into the question, the more difficult
it becomes to accept Mr Bailey's analysis. Is it, for instance,
so certain that before one can be ranked as a great poet
one's 'vision'—as Mr Bailey puts it—must 'take in the
whole of life'? Doubtless the greatest productions of the
human mind do possess this quality of universality; it is
present in *King Lear*, for example, and in the Book of Job.
But is it present in *Paradise Lost*? And does it follow,
because Wordsworth is more universal in his outlook than
Milton, that for that reason Wordsworth is the greater
poet? The most ardent Wordsworthian would hardly
subscribe to such a doctrine; and if the test of universal
vision breaks down in the case of Milton, it cannot be
safely applied to the case of Racine, or of anyone else. To
take one other of the qualities which, in Mr Bailey's view,
are indispensable to great poetry, and which Racine is
without—'the element of fine surprise'. How can we be
sure that Racine is not an exception to the rule, and that,
in fact, it is not one of his chief claims to distinction that
he can do without surprises? Surprises involve, by their
very nature, the use of detail; and the use of detail was
banished from Racine's art. He works, almost alone among
poets, by means of the most general conceptions, the most
ordinary terms; and with these he produces effects—*pace*
Mr Bailey—of the most amazing beauty and the subtlest
power. When Shakespeare wishes, for instance, to give
the suggestion of a silent night—how does he do it? By
the use of detail. 'Not a mouse stirring,' says Francisco
in the opening scene of *Hamlet*, and the thing is done.
Racine's method is totally different:

'Mais tout dort, et l'armée, et les vents, et Neptune.'

Here are a few ordinary words, the vague '*armée*' and the
simple '*vents*' and the commonplace generalized 'Neptune'; but what an impression of silence, of loneliness,
of darkness, of vastness, they bring before the mind.

8

Mr Bailey's ears, however, attuned to the music of Shakespeare, have been unable to detect the beauty of Racine's unfamiliar harmonies. This is unfortunate, for Racine, more than any other French poet, stands in need of an English interpreter; and it might have been hoped that Mr Bailey, with his rare interpretative gift, would have performed the function.

December 21, 1907

The Age of Louis XIV*

THE period covered by the fifth volume of *The Cambridge Modern History* possesses a unity and a dramatic interest which, if we except the Napoleonic era, are unequalled in the annals of modern Europe. Even more, perhaps, than the age of Napoleon, that of Louis XIV is remarkable for its wealth of startling incidents and conspicuous personages: such spectacular events as the revolutions in Holland and in England, the flight of the Huguenots, the rise and the humiliation of France; such dominant and boldly contrasted characters as—to mention only a few—William III and the Grand Pensionary, Milton and Charles II, Marlborough and his Duchess, and the 'Roi Soleil' himself—these must produce upon the minds of all who contemplate this great period an effect of glow and movement and colour akin to that of some vast and splendid decoration by Rubens or Veronese. And, no less than in a masterpiece of art, it is easy to perceive amid the mass of varied detail a single underlying subject which interpenetrates and gives meaning to the whole. The age might be summarized after the manner of an Elizabethan chronicle-play as *The Tragedy of Louis the Great*; for it is round the history of Louis that the rest of the action groups itself, and that history possesses all the essential characteristics of tragic development—the grandeur,

The Cambridge Modern History. Planned by the late Lord Acton, LL.D. Edited by A. W. Ward, Litt.D., G. W. Prothero, Litt.D., Stanley Leathes, M.A. Vol. V., *The Age of Louis XIV*. Cambridge: at the University Press.

the περιπέτεια, and the final ruin, inevitably following from what had gone before. Nor is the superhuman element wanting—the presence of issues more stupendous than any that can be summed up in the life of a man, the death-struggle of irreconcilable ideals and forces immeasurably great. It is difficult to believe that any book constructed out of such materials as these could fail to be interesting; yet it must be confessed that the present volume has achieved this almost impossible feat. By some mysterious process it has converted the excitement and the significance of the seventeenth century into flatness and insipidity. The learned authors remind one of the barbarians of the Dark Ages who used the masterpieces of antique sculpture for the building of common walls. How many priceless facts have gone to the making of one of their commonplace pages? As one looks closer one begins to discern between the lines some mutilated marble torso, or, here and there among the rubble, the fragments of a Juno's face. This failure may doubtless be explained to a great extent by the uninspiring effects of divided authorship; but perhaps an even more potent cause is the scale upon which the history has been written. The book falls between two stools; it should have been either a great deal longer or a great deal more condensed. As a rule, there are only two kinds of history which can be read with pleasure —the minutely detailed narrative, such as those of Tacitus and Macaulay, where events may be followed almost from day to day with the same sense of vividness and developing excitement as that which exists in real life; and the broad generalized outline of conditions and tendencies, such as those of Montesquieu and Michelet. To combine these styles, and so to produce an effect at once of breadth and of detail, required the consummate art and the immense knowledge of a Gibbon—qualities which have never come together in the same man either before or since. The volume before us, so far from resembling the *Decline and Fall*, lacks both virtues; it is not large enough for any real amplitude of narrative, while, on the other hand, it is without the cohesion and certainty of intention which might have been present in a smaller and less ambitious work. The ordinary reader will find those parts of it most profitable which are concerned with special subjects of isolated or general import, such as Mr Tanner's review of the naval administration of the later Stuarts, and the chapters on the Gallican Church and the development of science by Lord St Cyres and the late Sir Michael Foster. The contributions in literary history are far less happy. The somewhat irrelevant discussion of English Restoration literature contains nothing that is either illuminating or fresh, and M. Faguet in his article on the contemporary literature of France and its European influence—a subject teeming with interest and of the deepest significance—has given us merely commonplaces, when he might have given us a glimpse into the true spirit of the *grand siècle*. Indeed, to obtain this it is wiser to turn at once to Voltaire's *Siècle de Louis XIV*, which, incorrect and out of date as it is, yet produces upon the reader some feeling of the swell and movement of a great epoch. The ponderous *Cambridge History*, with its dry learning and scrupulous exactitude, bears the same relation to Voltaire's delicate little work as that of a full-length photograph to a rapid water-colour sketch by a master hand.

'The system of absolute government, which Louis steadily carried on during more than half a century,' was, as the editors observe in their preface, 'characteristic of the whole age.' But to say that Louis's government was absolute is not to say very much; the government of Frederick the Great was absolute, and so is that of the British in India; yet it would be preposterous to put the rule of Louis in the same class as these. His peculiar form of absolutism was distinguished by being intensely personal and supremely static, and it had its embodiment in the

château of Versailles. *The Cambridge History*, characteristi-
cally enough, only refers to Versailles once or twice,
incidentally, as if it had been nothing more than an
ordinary place of residence for the King; whereas a
complete chapter of minute description would not have
been too much to have given up to it, for in reality it was
the pivot upon which the whole epoch turned. Versailles,
with its interminable ceremonial, its colossal splendours,
its superhuman waterworks, its transplanted forests, its
heaped-up concentration of wealth and beauty, was the
real problem of the age. Was Versailles to be the type and
summit of European civilization, or was it not? That,
ultimately, was the question which brought William of
Orange to the throne of England, and ranged the bat-
talions at Blenheim. It was the spirit of Versailles—
arrogant, brilliant, and conventional—which gave its
glory to the reign of Louis, and guided the most fatal and
sinister of his acts—the invasion of Holland and the
revocation of the Edict of Nantes. And at the crisis of the
reign, when Louis had to decide whether he would accept
for his grandson the heritage of the Spanish Empire, or
renounce it and keep to his engagements, the same spirit,
to use Shakespeare's phrase, 'suggested' him still. Professor
Wolfgang Michael in his account of the affair, which
follows very closely indeed that given in M. Legrelle's
monumental but uninspired work, brushes aside the stories
told by Saint-Simon and Voltaire of the momentous
Council meetings held in Madame de Maintenon's sitting-
room, and concludes that Louis was actuated throughout
merely by reasons of State. But when we read Professor
Michael's complacent assertion—'Such were the motives
that induced King Louis to accept the will and to break
the Treaty'—it is difficult not to feel that he has forgotten
Versailles. Does not Voltaire's story, heightened though it
may have been, represent the profound truth that Louis
was unable from the whole bent of his character to resist

the pressure of his own dynastic ambitions, of the flattery of a Court, and the cajolery of a superstitious woman? Can Professor Michael seriously affirm that no thoughts or feelings save those of policy were present in the mind of Louis when, as Saint-Simon tells us, he surveyed with all the pride of majesty his assembled courtiers and exclaimed, pointing to his grandson: 'Voilà le Roi d'Espagne'?

If Versailles was the local habitation of the spirit which animated Louis, it is hardly fanciful to imagine that the spirit which opposed, and finally triumphed over, his dwelt somewhere among the grimy streets of the City of London, where the Mint was being reorganized and the Bank of England was beginning to exist. It was with Somers and with Montagu, with Newton and with Locke —the apostles of science and toleration—that the future lay. Though, as in most tragedies, the actual *dénouement* came through an accident—the genius of Marlborough— the splendid obscurantism of Louis, with its territorial ambitions and financial incompetence, was doomed from the first moment that it came into contact with freedom of thought combined with the command of the sea. Such a combination was bound to triumph, and the fact that the triumph was so complete is apt to blind our eyes to the true nature of the ideals which received their death blow at Blenheim. To us, who are the heirs of the glorious Revolution, Versailles and all that it involved means primarily something superficial, oppressive, and base; but, after all, it meant more than that to a generation of noble and gifted men. It meant a great ideal—an ideal of decoration and of pride, of perfections more than human and of majesty that deemed itself almost divine. Its immortal part lives still for us in the poetry of Racine and in the prose of Bossuet and La Bruyère. Not far from Paris its mortal remains are to be found. The empty illimitable palace amid its deserted gardens and its fountains that play no more has been preserved to us, cold and rigid in Time's strata, like the fossil of some vast and mysterious monster of an abolished world.

April 11, 1908

Molière*

ENGLISHMEN have always loved Molière. He is one of the very few French writers whom we can explore without the uneasy feeling of being in a foreign country; we are at home with him, and he, we feel, is at home with us. We have, too, given solid proof of our admiration, for there is no other foreign author whom we have imitated so much. Ever since he wrote he has dominated our comic stage. 'The frippery of crucified Molière,' as Pope put it, has always been the stock-in-trade of the hack English playwright; and some of the most famous scenes of Sheridan and Congreve have been 'lifted' almost bodily from the author of the *Misanthrope* and the *Femmes Savantes*. The new edition of his plays, prepared, with an English translation, by Mr A. R. Waller, affords a fresh opportunity to English readers of renewing—or beginning—a delightful acquaintance. Mr Waller's object in making the translation has been, he tells us, to meet the requirements of 'those who, having some slight knowledge of French, might find a rendering in simple modern English, side by side with the French text, not unacceptable as a helpful companion in case of need.' A translator is always a bold man. 'Que diable allait-il faire dans cette galère?' is the inevitable question which rises to the lips of every reader, and proves more often than not unanswerable. Mr Waller is particularly courageous; for he is translating Molière; and he is translating him with the original on the opposite page.

* *The Plays of Molière.* In French, with an English Translation and Notes by A. R. Waller, and an Introduction by George Saintsbury. 8 vols. Edinburgh: John Grant.

'Translating Molière,' says Mr Meredith, 'is like humming an air one has heard performed by an accomplished violinist of the pure tones without flourish'; and Mr Waller has not been afraid to put the pure tones of Molière on one page, and his own hummings on the other. No one, of course, could expect the hummings to rival the pure tones; but one might reasonably have hoped that, since Mr Waller has chosen to hum, he should at least do so in tune with his original. Unfortunately, Mr Waller's translation is not only flat, it is also inaccurate. To those who have only 'some slight knowledge of French' his version will, in too many cases, come as a stumbling-block rather than an aid. It would be easy to multiply instances, but one example will be sufficient to indicate the perfunctory manner in which Mr Waller has performed a task which deserved the most unremitting care and the most scrupulous correction. Sganarelle, in the *Festin de Pierre*, winds up his argument in favour of the providential nature of the universe by a practical demonstration of the exquisite contrivance of the human mechanism. 'How wonderful to be able to move just as one wishes! Look at me! I can clap my hands, bow my head, swing my legs, turn my body——' and in his excitement he turns too quickly and falls flat upon the ground. 'Bon! Voilà ton raisonnement qui a le nez cassé' (And now your argument has got a broken nose) is Don Juan's admirable comment. But how does this appear in Mr Waller's translation? 'Good, so your argument has broken your nose.' The reader who mistakes that feeble sentence for the sparkling thought of Molière must have a very 'slight knowledge of French' indeed.

The extreme laxity (to use no stronger word) of Mr Waller's rendering is particularly disappointing, since the quality of Molière's genius shows itself nowhere more clearly than in his exquisite precision. Whatever his point may be—and one might compile an infinite gradation of

his points, ranging from the broadest buffoonery to the
subtlest psychological crux—he can seize it and make the
best of it with the same unerring exactitude, the same
undeviating certainty of touch. Mr Meredith's metaphor
of the 'pure tones without flourish' is no empty one, for
Molière's best phrases have precisely the rich simplicity
of the *virtuoso*. He can call up with a common sentence
a whole universe of reverberating suggestion and pervasive
irony. '*Nous avons changé tout cela!*'—It is the epitome of all
the cranks of the world. He can make a bad pun the
instrument of eternal mockery. 'Veux-tu toute la vie
offenser la grammaire?' the pedantic lady furiously asks
her servant, and the country wench replies in all gravity:
'Qui parle d'offenser grand'mère ni grand-pere?' Is not
that the last word on the subject? To read one of his scenes
is to watch some wonderful cook at work over a delicious
dish—keeping it on the simmer while each savoury
ingredient is dropped in: the oil, the olive, the salt—and
then at the psychological moment whipping it off the fire,
and setting it before you done to a turn. In short, Molière's
workmanship is essentially classical. It is true that his
construction is apt to be weak; the action of his plays is
too often 'huddled up', as Professor Saintsbury says in his
introduction to the present edition; but the pervading
spirit of his work is none the less that very spirit of
precision, finish, and refinement which informs all that is
most characteristic in the art of his countrymen. But it is
the great distinction of Molière that he is not only a
classicist, but something else besides. The weakness of the
classical ideal lies in its tendency towards the narrow and
the confined—towards a perfection which is only perfect
because it has excluded and ignored so much. Pushed to its
extremity, it produces a Voltaire—the most consummate
of artists, dancing in a vacuum on the tight-rope of his own
wit; and its antithesis is to be found among the dramas of
the romantic Elizabethans, whose looseness, vagueness,

disorder, and irregularity are redeemed by the image of large and tumultuous life which those very qualities have brought into being. The marvellous achievement of Molière was to combine the polished brilliance of the classic with the romantic's sense of humanity. He is as definite, as witty, as complete as Voltaire himself; and yet his pages are throbbing with vitality; his characters stream across them in all the freshness and in all the variety of life;his world is the great world—the world of Shakespeare and Cervantes, of Balzac and Scott.

But if this combination of breadth and refinement is the distinctive feature of Molière's art, what is the distinctive feature of Molière himself? What, to use Professor Saintsbury's expression, is the 'essence' of Molière? In his introduction Professor Saintsbury discusses the question, and discusses it with all his usual vivacity and learning; everything that he says is interesting; and it is only to be regretted that so much of what he says should be also a little perverse. One cannot help being reminded of the lines of Célimène:

> 'Le sentiment d'autrui n'est jamais pour lui plaire:
> Il prend toujours en main l'opinion contraire,
> Et penserait paraître un homme du commun
> Si l'on voyait qu'il fût de l'avis de quelqu'un.'

Most modern critics have laid stress on the serious side of Molière's mind; Professor Saintsbury has taken up *l'opinion contraire*, and argues forcibly that Molière was at heart a laugher, and nothing more. He was 'the Master of the Laugh'. His 'essence' simply 'asks everything which suggests itself, "Can you help me to make men laugh?" and if so, it takes the thing, and makes it do this. With the rest it *n'a que faire*, as the French phrase goes.' Surely that is as paradoxical as any of the exaggerated statements about Molière's sole value lying in his tragic power. No one in his senses will doubt for a minute that Molière was

indeed 'the Master of the Laugh'. But was he (as Professor
Saintsbury declares) master of nothing more? Was he not
also the Master of the Smile? Is not that, in fact, his true
'essence'? Laughter is the expression of a simple emotion;
but a smile (no less than a tear) is an intellectual thing;
and Molière's greatest work is intellectual to an intense
degree. The distinction is nowhere more plainly visible
than in one of the best known of all his comedies—*Le
Bourgeois Gentilhomme*. The latter half of that delightful
piece is a cataract of rollicking buffoonery, which leaves
one with aching sides, gasping for breath. Professor
Saintsbury's words exactly fit it; Moliére has taken the
foolish tradesman playing the *grand seigneur*, and has
covered him with such enormous ridicule, has plunged
him into such preposterous predicaments, that men will
laugh over him till the end of time. And if Moliére's sole
object had been to do that—to draw the greatest possible
quantity of laughter from his subject—all that was necessary was to write the whole play on the same pattern and
the thing was done. But that was not his sole object, for
the earlier scenes present a complete contrast to the later
ones; it is not their laughableness that makes them
valuable, but their psychology. The Monsieur Jourdain
whom we love and know, the Monsieur Jourdain whom
Molière has drawn for us so exquisitely, so subtly, so
sympathetically—at him we can hardly laugh at all, at
him we must perpetually smile. And who can doubt that a
creation such as that is really a finer and a greater achievement than the most triumphant evocation of the most
Olympian laughter? Professor Saintsbury, indeed, is
forced into strange extremes by his theory, for he has to do
his best to turn each of Molière's most profound and
complex character-studies into something funny, something that will 'help to make men laugh'. He has to make
excuses for Don Juan (who is never even ridiculous);
he has to shuffle aside Tartufe (who is nearly always

horrible); he has to forget Harpagon altogether. 'Hélas!
mon pauvre argent! mon pauvre argent! mon cher ami!
on m'a privé de toi; et, puisque tu m'es enlevé, j'ai perdu
mon support, ma consolation, ma joie; tout est fini pour
moi, et je n'ai plus que faire au monde.' That is despair;
and despair, surely, is no laughing matter. Over the
Misanthrope Professor Saintsbury fights a gallant fight; but
it is impossible to believe that any reader who is acquainted
with that wonderful drama will be convinced by his
arguments. For, indeed, there is no escaping the fact that
in the *Misanthrope* at least Molière is not only supremely
gay and supremely brilliant, but supremely melancholy
too. The play is a tragedy in the truest sense of the word,
though there is no 'sceptred pall' in it, no Shakespearean
imagination, no Sophoclean grandeur; it is the tragedy
of actual life. Its climax does not come in death, but in a
lady leaving a room. And when that happens, when at
the last, amid the silence of the little *salon*, Célimène,
without a word, turns round and passes out for ever from
our sight—who does not feel the same quality of anguish,
the same poignancy of desolation, as that which fills us
when King Oedipus goes forth into the darkness, or
Cordelia dies?

October 26, 1907

Seventeenth-Century Criticism*

THE critical work of the seventeenth century deserves more respect and attention than it usually receives, and Professor Spingarn's collection of the literary essays of the period is a welcome step towards the fuller appreciation of a brilliant and fascinating age. Professor Spingarn's introduction is an illuminating piece of work, laying down the main lines of his subject with admirable clarity, and following them up with real force and insight and that rare kind of erudition which never grows pedantic. The essays themselves are interesting from many points of view. The fact that they include none of the work of Dryden—whose critical essays, edited by Professor Ker, form two companion volumes in the same series—is not without its advantages, though it is true that the criticism of the seventeenth century without Dryden puts one in mind of the play of *Hamlet* without the Prince of Denmark. Dryden undoubtedly ranks as one of the great critics of the world. In all the qualities peculiarly essential to criticism—sympathy, discrimination, breadth of outlook, and power of exposition—he far surpassed his contemporaries, and he possessed the crowning grace of an exquisite prose style. Yet it is sometimes worth while to put on one side the giants of an age, and to consider those smaller figures of the second and the third rank who represent the intelligent public opinion of their generation. Sometimes the giant so far overtops his fellows that his head is lost among the

Critical Essays of the Seventeenth Century. Edited by J. E. Spingarn, Adjunct Professor of Comparative Literature, Columbia University, New York. 3 vols. Vols. I and II. Oxford: at the Clarendon Press.

clouds and his prophecies pass unheeded. But in the present instance this was not the case. Professor Spingarn's extracts prove conclusively that the main current of seventeenth-century thought was flowing in precisely the direction which Dryden himself was pointing out; and it is at least possible that even if Dryden had never lived the same results would have followed. In any case, the fact that the great mass of enlightened taste in England did change so completely and so consciously during the course of the century is of the highest interest. It gives to Professor Spingarn's volumes something of the glamour of romance. We are shown the beginnings of a new idea, timid at first and fluctuating, then gradually strengthening, at last triumphant and supreme; an immense revolution has been accomplished; and the century which knew Shakespeare in his prime has become the nurse of Pope.

To our own generation these essays should be particularly interesting, because they give expression to a view of literature which is altogether opposed to those of the present day. On the subject of Shakespeare, for instance, we find Thomas Rymer in his review of *Othello* declaring: 'There is not a monkey but understands nature better, not a pug in Barbary that has not a truer taste of things.' To us this is nonsense, and blasphemous nonsense. Yet Rymer was neither a fool nor a brute; he was a clever man whose opinions were highly respected by his contemporaries, and who was pronounced by Pope to have been, 'on the whole, one of the best critics we ever had.' What is the explanation of this? How is it possible that a sensible man could ever have given utterance to such stuff, and that other sensible men tolerated it for a moment? The answer is that even the best judge of wine will lose his palate for port after drinking nothing but madeira, and that the later critics of the seventeenth century were in a similar situation. They had become fascinated and obsessed by an ideal of beauty so completely alien to that of the Elizabethans that even abuse of the masterpieces of Shakespeare seemed to them neither outrageous nor absurd. What this new ideal of beauty was receives ample illustration in the present volumes. Perhaps it was never summed up more concisely than in Sir John Denham's famous apostrophe to the Thames at Cooper's Hill:

> 'Oh, could I flow like thee, and make thy stream
>   My great example, as it is my theme!
> Though deep, yet clear; though gentle, yet not dull;
> Strong without rage, without o'erflowing full.'

It was an ideal of lucidity and order and polish, of easy majesty and finely discriminated sense. Undoubtedly it received a powerful impetus from the example of France, whose literature, with the establishment of the Academy and the rise of Corneille, was entering upon its most characteristic phase; and the eventual triumph of the new school became assured during the exile at Paris of the English Court, with its poets and men of letters, before the Restoration. Equally strong was the force of the natural reaction against the decaying traditions of the Elizabethan age. Literary schools, no less than nations, have their mysterious periods of growth and of decline, and the great literature which Spenser and Donne had started on its victorious career guttered out amid the unformed diffuseness and the incredible contortions of those strange 'Caroline poets', whose works have lately been brought to light by Professor Saintsbury after centuries of oblivion. It was only to have been expected that men of intelligence and taste should have rebelled against the poetic system of a Benlowes, according to whom the souls in hell 'frying freeze, and freezing fry', or of the amazing *Pharonnida*—a poem so immense and so entangled that the author forgets the name of his own hero in the course of it. Besides these influences, we must take into account that unexplained law by which the poetic inspiration of an age seems to follow what may be called, for want of a better term, a nation's 'centre of gravity'. With the Elizabethans the centre of gravity was among the middle classes—the country gentlemen like Drake and Raleigh, the country yeomen like Shakespeare, and the University scholars like Marlowe and Ben Jonson. After the Restoration the centre of gravity moved more and more rapidly towards the aristocracy, until at the beginning of the eighteenth century it became fixed in the great Whig families who had achieved the Revolution. And simultaneously literature took on the qualities of aristocracy, grew refined, brilliant, and ordered, and concerned itself exclusively with the life of London drawing-rooms. In fact, the new ideals which governed literature were the ideals of 'high society'. The emphasis which critics belonging to this school laid upon the 'rules' of Aristotle, the 'three unities', and the rest of the pseudo-classical conventions is, as Professor Spingarn points out, somewhat delusive, for the real foundation for the new spirit was to be found in the present, and not in the past. When Samuel Butler exclaimed in his pungent doggerel that, according to the critics of his day:

'Not an actor shall presume to squeek
Unless he have a license for't in Greek,
Nor Whittington henceforward sell his cat in
Plain vulgar English, without mewing Latin,'

he was arguing beside the point. It was not because of their antiquity that the new critical school adopted the Aristotelian formulae, but because they seemed to fit in with an ideal of literature which was pre-eminently, as the phrase went, 'correct'. This was the attitude of the majority of the critics, from Dryden downwards. The Elizabethans, with their imaginative exaltation, their 'wild enormities', their adventurous intensity of spirit, seemed uncouth and barbarous, and even shocking, to minds completely penetrated with the beauties of refinement and restraint. The general view, indeed, was less uncompromising than Rymer's; the elder dramatists were, on the whole, in a somewhat shamefaced way, admired in spite of their 'faults'. Dryden's praise of Shakespeare, with all its qualifications, is passionate and splendid; and lesser men followed where Dryden led. 'Shakespeare and Fletcher,' says Sheffield, 'are the wonders now':

> 'Consider them and read them o'er and o'er,
> Go see them played, then read them as before.
> For though in many things they grossly fail,
> Over our passions still they so prevail
> That our own grief by theirs is rocked asleep,
> The dull are forced to feel, the wise to weep.'

That is a fine panegyric, and yet, clearly enough, it has been extorted by the feelings against the dictates of the intellect. 'In many things' Shakespeare 'grossly fails'! Sheffield's attitude suggests that of a man of fashion towards some country milkmaid whose beauty was too magnificent not to be admired; but, without a hoop and without a fan, with such an open-air complexion and such an untrammelled gait—she could never be presented at Whitehall!

May 2, 1908

The Author of 'Hudibras' *

SAMUEL BUTLER—'a man,' as Dr Johnson says, 'whose name can only perish with his language'—is one of the obscurest figures in English literature. Not only are the circumstances of his life almost entirely unknown, but those general qualities of mind which enable us to image, however vaguely, the rough outline of a character seem in his case to have left very few traces behind them. Butler lives now merely as the author of *Hudibras*; but the author of *Hudibras* is an indeterminate personage, of whom nothing more can be said with certainty than that he was an extraordinarily witty, eminently sensible, and some-what brutal man. There is a tradition that his life was unfortunate, that his talents were admired and neglected, and that he was allowed to die in poverty by the ungrateful Charles II. But one wishes to know more. How did the pungent satirist bear his sorrows? Did he laugh or did he weep? What was his philosophy? What was his true attitude towards the world? From this point of view the volume now published by the Cambridge University Press, containing a collection of Butler's prose writings, is of the greatest interest. It is made up of a large number of 'Characters', after the manner of Theophrastus, and a mass of observations and notes, written in varying degrees of elaboration, upon a multitude of miscellaneous topics. The majority of the Characters and a small selection of the notes have been already printed; the rest are repro-duced for the first time from the manuscripts in the British

Samuel Butler: Characters and Passages from Note-Books. Edited by A. R. Waller, M.A. Cambridge: at the University Press.

Museum. It is in the notes that the main interest of the volume lies. Butler's Characters are crammed full of thought and observation; they are admirably written and vigorously conceived; yet they fail to hold the attention of the modern reader. Doubtless this is owing in part to the extremely topical nature of the subject-matter. Butler describes with endless wit and gusto 'a Huffing Courtier', 'a Fifth-Monarchy Man', 'a Fantastic', 'a Melancholy Man', 'an Amorist', 'a Virtuoso', but such figures are curiously unreal to us, and this effect is heightened by his method of vituperative caricature. His portraits are so singular and so savage that, do what we will, we cannot believe in the existence of the originals. And, in addition, their very wealth of matter proves a stumbling-block. The mind is over-burdened by the serried succession of ideas, the immense accumulation of images. Some of the characters—'an Hypocritical Nonconformist', 'a Modern Politician', 'an Astrologer'—come near to being prose versions of well-known passages in *Hudibras*; but they lack the sprightliness of Butler's octosyllables and the fantastic fun which flashes and explodes in his preposterous rhymes. One is tempted to believe that English prose is too heavy an instrument for this kind of writing. Clarendon alone, perhaps, who had the advantage of drawing from the life, has succeeded in our literature as a prose portrait-painter; but how far even his fine and sympathetic studies fall below the fiery presentments of Saint-Simon or the brilliant profiles of La Bruyère!

The 'Miscellaneous Observations and Reflections on Various Subjects', by far the greater number of which are now printed for the first time, are not only, owing to their occasional nature, less overloaded with thought than the characters, but they possess the additional interest of throwing a great deal of light upon the habit of mind of the writer. These intimate and random jottings, most of them cast into an epigrammatic form, a few developed into brilliant little essays, leave the reader under a vivid impression of Butler's personality. The impression is highly interesting; but whether it is equally pleasant is more open to doubt. They reveal a mind of amazing acuteness and power—there is hardly a single dull or commonplace sentence in these two hundred pages; but it is a mind which never excites and, except through its perfect efficiency, never charms. Butler's intelligence was intensely positive. Though it is true that he lampooned the Royal Society, his cast of thought was scientific, and several pages of the present collection are devoted to his memoranda upon facts and theories relating to the physical world. But it was in the world of men that his powers of vivid observation and searching analysis found their fullest scope. He was a bitter and fearless sceptic, whose eye penetrated into every cranny and whose hand tore off every veil. No one was ever less of a dupe to the deceitful outsides of humanity. 'The more silly and ridiculous things are in themselves,' he exclaims, 'the more sacred and solemn pretences they require to set them off.' And again:

'The saint and the hypocrite are so very like, that they pass all the world over undistinguished: the difference being only in the Inside, of which we have no guess (until it be too late) but by symptoms that commonly belie both. All we are sure of is that the hypocrites are the greater number, more devoutly zealous in appearance, and much more crafty than those that are in earnest.'

In every department of life he found the same pretences, the same emptiness, and the same gullibility: doctors, soldiers, lawyers, all alike were infected:

'The most difficult professions in the world,' he says, 'are the easiest to be assumed and with less study practiced by impostures and men of the weakest parts, as divinity, politics, commands in war, physic, poetry, &c., while the meanest and merely mechanical are never to be attained without great labour and pains. So the greater any employment is the easier it is to be performed.'

He reserved the fiercest of his invectives for the pretences of religion. Here are some of them:

'There is no folly or madness so vain and ridiculous, but if it put itself into the protection of piety and religion is by the easy, credulous and ignorant reputed sacred and not to be touched.'

'When the Devil tempted Christ, he set him on the highest pinnacle of the Temple. Great church preferments are great temptations.'

'The Church of Rome teaches the people religion as men teach singing birds; shut them up and keep them dark.'

'They call confession purging of the soul, and they use it commonly as men take purges—to get a better stomach to their sins.'

'In all religions, for one proselyte that is made by preaching, there are hundreds that are converted by private tamperings and particular interests.'

There are countless indications among these notes that Butler was a truly religious man; but his disgust at the hypocrites and sectaries of his age urged him to a bitterness of expression which sometimes wears the appearance of complete scepticism. He attacks every side at once: 'The papists say they believe as the Church believes, and the protestants laugh at them for it, but they do the very same thing themselves; all the difference is, the first believe by wholesale, and the last by retail.' No doubt the following sentence sums up the feelings which dictated these outbursts: 'There is nothing that can prevail more to persuade a man to be an atheist as to see such unreasonable beasts pretend to religion.' Swift might have said the same thing.

Indeed, throughout these reflections one is constantly reminded of the great Dean of St Patrick's. Butler, like Swift, seems never to be really comfortable unless he is exposing some stupidity or some wickedness; his mind naturally inclined towards the consideration of the frailties of humanity, just as Milton's turned towards the sublime, and Keats's towards the beautiful. Like Swift, too, Butler has all the bitter arrogance of a great man who has failed in life. His diagnosis of the fools of this world is inexhaustible; he pursues them into every hiding-place; he depicts them in every attitude and under every light; he scorns them in the rabble; he mocks them in high places. 'Fools and knaves'—that is his final verdict on humanity—only 'there are more fools than knaves in the world, else the knaves would not have enough to live upon.' 'The reason,' he concludes, 'why fools and knaves thrive better in the world than wiser and honester men is because they are nearer to the general temper of mankind, which is nothing but a mixture of cheat and folly.' Such reflections are far from cheerful; and Butler was perfectly conscious of the gloom of his philosophy. Again and again his pessimism comes out, undisguised and unmitigated, in these curious pages:

'The world is so vile a thing, that Providence commonly makes fools and knaves happy, and good men miserable in it, to let us know there is no great difference between happiness and misery here.'

'All the pleasures of luxury or avarice, or any other delightful vice, and the greatest parts of all the employments and business of this world, serve only to divert man from reflecting too much upon the misery, frailty, and vanity of his condition in this world, and the horrid conclusion of all—Death.'

But though there is much bitterness and much melancholy in Butler's self-revelations, there is never a trace of agitation, horror, or despair. It is here that he differs from his successor; he has none of the terrific passion, none of the *saeva indignatio*, which inspires and elevates the pessimism of Swift. Butler was without Swift's grandeur of soul, and thus the final effect which these writings produce is disappointing. One has come into contact with a mind of great strength, brilliance, and penetration, but without a spark of nobility; a genius which can run and leap and wrestle, but which never soars. We might almost fancy him—such was his overpowering sanity—jeering at Swift himself, and asking him if the human race, after all, was worth losing one's temper over. There is something a little terrifying in the thought of the poor, deserted, worn-out, caustic man, with the large hard face the old pictures show us, waiting so grimly in his sordid London lodgings for 'the horrid conclusion of all'. 'I do now begin,' he jotted down in his note-book, 'to find myself naturally inclined to cast up an accompt with Death, what the true value of anything really comes to.' One can guess well enough what the 'accompt' would have been like—a long list of follies and vanities and deceptions on one side, and a little wit on the other.

February 6, 1909

D. Later Literature

Jonathan Swift*

MR TEMPLE SCOTT's valuable edition of Swift's prose works, begun nearly twelve years ago, is now completed by the present volume, the twelfth, which contains a full bibliography of Swift's writings, essays on his portraits and his relations with Stella, and a general index to the whole work. The completion of this edition is an event of real importance to all those who have the interests of our literature at heart, for though the most popular of Swift's works have been endlessly reprinted, the whole body of his achievement has not been put before the public since the edition prepared by Sir Walter Scott at the beginning of the last century. Thus in giving to the world an authoritative and scholarly version of the most important of Swift's writings—his prose works—Mr Temple Scott has done no small service to English letters. The interesting bibliography in the volume before us, compiled by Mr Spencer Jackson, which describes 'all the editions of Swift's writings, whether separate or collected, published before the end of the eighteenth century', is in itself sufficient to give Mr Scott's edition a unique value to students of Swift. It is to be hoped that these volumes will be speedily followed by the edition of the correspondence which is to form a companion to the prose works, and that in due time a reprint of the whole of Swift's verse will complete an admirable undertaking.

The Prose Works of Jonathan Swift, D.D. Edited by Temple Scott. Vol. XII, Essays on the Portraits of Swift by Sir Frederick Falkiner, and on Swift and Stella by the Very Rev. the Dean of St Patrick's. Bibliography of Swift's Works by W. Spencer Jackson, and a General Index. London: George Bell & Sons.

Swift was something more than a great writer, he was a
great man; and the interest attaching to his name has
always depended as much upon his character as upon his
works. There are many indications that this was the case
among the general public even during his lifetime. Swift's
power, though for a few years it was enormous, was never
declared or obvious; he occupied no official position in
politics; as a public man he was a failure, and even his
deanery, when it came to him, was a fatal blow to his
ambitions. Yet, in spite of the comparative obscurity of his
career, his personal characteristics and his personal history
absorbed the attention of his contemporaries. A curious
proof of this may be found in Mr Jackson's bibliography,
which shows us that 'Cadenus and Vanessa', that strange
poem which at once reveals and conceals the secret of
Swift's relations with Hester Vanhomrigh, went into no
less than eight editions within the year of its publication.
The essay on Swift's portraits by the late Sir Frederick
Falkiner contains precisely similar evidence. The number
of these portraits, either copied or original, is so great that
'after a two years' hunt' it was found necessary 'to forgo
the hope of truly identifying half the "genuine" Swifts
in the homes and the collections of Ireland and England';
and this confusion has arisen not only from the multiplica-
tion of copies by unknown hands, but from the large
number of replicas made by the most eminent artists, to
whom, as Sir Frederick Falkiner tells us, 'the temptation
would seem often to have been irresistible to eke out their
income by a few repetitions on the sly'—so pressing was
the demand for portraits of the great Dean. Unfortunately,
however, the quantity of these portraits is no compensation
for their quality. Swift was never painted by a master,
and thus, though his features are familiar to everyone—the
high forehead, the arched nose, the arrogant lips, the eyes
'quite azure as the heavens', and the black terrific
eyebrows above them—yet they live for us on no supreme

canvas, and we are fain to do our best with our imagination to clothe with the force and fire of genius the dull presentments we possess. The most distinguished of the painters to whom Swift sat was Charles Jervas, who, if we are to believe tradition, was very far from considering himself the second-rate artist that he was. 'Poor little Tit,' he exclaimed on one occasion after having finished a copy of a Titian, 'how he would stare!' Jervas gave lessons in painting to Pope, who in his turn tried his hand at his friend's portrait. 'I find my hand most successful in drawing of friends,' Pope wrote to Caryll, 'insomuch that my masterpieces have been one of Dr Swift and one of Mr Betterton.' But the poet destroyed his paintings in despair. 'When St Luke painted,' he said, 'an angel came and finished the work, and it will be thought hereafter that when I painted, the devil put the last hand to my pieces.' Pope seems to have painted and written on the same principles.

Sir Frederick Falkiner regrets that Swift never sat to Hogarth—it would have been possible during his last visit to London in 1726—and goes on to draw a parallel between 'the Swift of the painters' and 'the Hogarth of the poets'. At first sight the comparison is attractive, but it grows less satisfactory the more one examines it. After all, Hogarth, though it is true that he was a satirist, was no misanthrope; his spirit was essentially cheerful and good-natured, and when he laughed he laughed outright. He knew nothing of the bitter mockery of Swift. To find in painting anything at all resembling the Yahoos and the Struldbrugs one must turn to the terrible visions of Goya, or to some of Daumier's overwhelming caricatures. But there is another even more vital difference: Hogarth's genius was fundamentally poetical, while Swift's was a prose genius through and through. If one were obliged to look for parallels among painters, surely there is only one master with whom, so far as style at least is concerned,

Swift can be fitly compared—Velazquez. Swift's writing
has all the restraint, all the economy of effort, all the
sobriety of tone, which fill the great Spaniard's pictures;
and it produces effects as brilliant and as unforgettable.
When we read his finest pages we experience sensations
such as those that are evoked by an 'Infanta' or a
'Philip IV'; we ask in vain by what magic those quiet and
commonplace ingredients have been converted into the
visible image of life and force. Swift's is the least emphatic
of styles, and the most powerful. His mind, infinitely
unpoetical, turned naturally towards the detailed, the dry,
and the material, discarding all the dazzling allurements
of fancy, and seeking its inspiration, often enough, in the
dirt. It relied for its effects upon its own strength, and upon
that alone. The only ornament in his writing is the
rhythm, so that, compared to the decorative and imaginative prose of such a writer as Sir Thomas Browne, it
resembles the naked body of an athlete beside some Prince
in gorgeous raiment. Who can say which is the more
beautiful? Who can balance the subtle vigour of nudity
against the splendour of glowing colour and elaborate
form? It is more fruitful to compare Swift with one of the
great masters in his own style—with Voltaire, for instance
—where we may find the same clarity and sobriety, the
same unerring precision of statement, the same pre-
occupation with the concrete and the real. Then perhaps
we shall understand more completely the true essence of
Swift's genius. What is it that distinguishes *Candide* from
the 'Modest Proposal for Preventing the Children of Poor
People from being a Burden to their Parents or the
Country'? Both are masterpieces of irony; both are
intensely serious; but the Frenchman attains his end by
means of a ghastly gaiety, while Swift employs a more
deadly weapon still—an impassive and unrelaxing gravity
which never fluctuates, which shrinks from nothing,
which advances rigidly and logically to the most pre-

posterous conclusions, and leaves us at last in an agony, as if the curtain had gone down on a tragic scene.

If it is true that an underlying sense of tragedy animates Swift's greatest work, it is equally certain that the same dreadful influence dominated his life. The story of his relations with 'Stella' and 'Vanessa' is reviewed once more in the present volume by Dr Bernard, the Dean of St Patrick's, who is able to contribute a new piece of evidence relating to the much-disputed question as to Swift's marriage—a letter written by the Bishop of Meath while both Swift and Stella were alive, mentioning their marriage as a fact. The importance of this letter lies in the support which it affords to a number of independent traditions of much later date. Thus it adds in some degree to the probability of the truth of the marriage; but the whole matter still remains within the region of doubtful speculation. There seems, indeed, very little reason to regret this. Whether Swift went through the ceremony of marriage or not is in reality a question of merely formal and antiquarian interest; whatever the answer, we shall be no nearer the central mystery of Swift's life. What was the nature of his feelings towards the two women whose fates were so strangely twisted round his own? What were the compelling forces, what were the crucial acts, of that tragedy? We shall never know more than we know at present, and that is so little that the most careful biographers are able to come to totally contrary conclusions upon the most important points at issue. Thus Sir Leslie Stephen inclined to believe that Swift was in love with Vanessa and not with Stella, while Dr Bernard is of opinion that he was in love with Stella and was never anything more than Vanessa's intimate friend. Whatever conclusion we may come to, however, it seems clear that we have no reason to condemn the conduct of any of the three. It is easy enough, for instance, to say with Dr Bernard that 'Swift was to blame for allowing Vanessa to lose her foolish heart to him'; but it is not so easy to say how he could have prevented it, or how, when it had once happened, he was to treat the situation. We know far too little of the facts to bring in any verdict but one of 'Not proven'.

February 27, 1909

Alexander Pope*

'THERE is a certain type of reader (more common than is generally supposed),' says 'George Paston', 'who, when the name of Pope is mentioned, exclaims: "Pope! That's the man who said, 'Whatever is is right.' " ' A little more searching of the memory, and he recalls that Pope was also responsible for such platitudes as 'The proper study of mankind is man' and 'An honest man's the noblest work of God'. He shows a tendency to confuse Pope with Solomon, and he has been known to attribute a line from the 'Essay on Man' to Shakespeare. It is to this type of reader that the author more especially dedicates the present 'plain chronicle of the life and work of the poet'; and to all such these two volumes, with their easy, unaffected style, their unstinted reproductions of Pope's most famous passages, and their numerous illustrations, may be heartily recommended. Readers to whom Pope's history and writings are more familiar will not be sorry to have the opportunity of reviewing once again the incidents of that singular and vexed career, and of refreshing their recollections of many of the finest verses in English literature. The biography would have gained if it had been less rambling, and if the main outlines of Pope's career had been more clearly indicated. Though some interesting unpublished correspondence has been collected, it is to be regretted that full use has not been made of the work of previous scholars. Particularly unfortunate is the omission

*Mr. Pope: his Life and Times by George Paston. With 26 Illustrations, including 2 Photogravure Frontispieces. 2 vols. London: Hutchinson & Co.

of any reference to Professor Lounsbury's elaborate
researches into the circumstances attending the publication of the early editions of the 'Dunciad'—researches
which have thrown much fresh light upon the extraordinarily tortuous methods employed by Pope in his
literary ventures. Examples of these methods are, however,
to be found in 'George Paston's' book; Pope's complicated
devices and deceptions relative to his correspondence are
alone sufficient to indicate the perverted temper of the
man. Young's lines on 'Julia' have often been applied to
him:

> 'For her own breakfast she'll project a scheme,
>   Nor take her tea without a stratagem.'

And in Pope's case it is clear enough that this crooked
habit of mind was simply one manifestation of that
deformed and sickly state of being which had dwarfed
and twisted his body, and made one 'long disease' of his
whole life. He was, in modern parlance, a *névrosé*. Abnor-
mally sensitive to stimuli, his frail organization responded
frantically to the slightest outward touch. If you looked
at him he would spit poison, and he would wind himself
into an endless meshwork of intrigues and suspicions if
you did not. But it was not only in malignity and contortions that Pope's sensitiveness showed itself; throughout
his life he gave proof of a tenderness which was something
more than a merely selfish susceptibility, and of a power
of affection as unmistakable as his power of hate. In spite
of hysterical bickerings and downright quarrels, his
relations with the Blounts were animated by a sincere
and generous friendship; with all his egoism and vanity,
he never lost his profound admiration for the only one of
his contemporaries who was as great a writer as himself—
Swift; and his devotion to his mother forms one of the
most touching episodes in the whole history of letters.

These characteristics are expressed with remarkable distinctness in all the well-known portraits of Pope, especially in the fine Kneller reproduced in the present work, where the poet's face, with the large eyes and quivering mouth, seems to be the battle-ground of discordant emotions the intensity of which is the intensity of disease. And precisely similar qualities are to be found stamped on every page of Pope's poetry. Why it is that this fact should be persistently ignored by the great majority of readers is one of the puzzles of criticism; but it is certain that, whatever view may be held of Pope's character, his works are almost universally regarded as examples of cold, lifeless, and unimpassioned writing. One reason for this is, no doubt, as 'George Paston' suggests, that habit of trite moralizing which Pope shared with his age, and which produces upon the casual reader an impression of conventionality and insincerity. But perhaps a more potent cause of mis-understanding is the form in which Pope wrote. How is it possible that verse so regular, so ordered, so scrupulously exact, so 'smooth', as the eighteenth-century phrase went, should be the language of passion? Everyone knows that passion is a rough, disordered, fitful thing, chafing at artificial rules, and bending the stiff conventions of verse-making to its own vigorous and unexpected purposes; the true vehicle for passion is the varied blank verse of the Elizabethans, not the even couplet of Pope. These considerations, true enough in general, only serve to prove in Pope's particular case that he was an artist of supreme genius; for they simply show—if they show anything—that he succeeded in expressing passion, not by means of his medium, but in spite of it. But, after all, the whole conception of Pope as an infinitely careful craftsman —a laborious inlayer and polisher, whose method of work precluded by its very nature the fervour of inspiration—is a mistaken one. Pope certainly devoted an immense amount of labour to the perfecting of his compositions, more, perhaps, than any other of our great poets, save

Keats and Milton; but it does not follow from this that his writing was devoid of the 'fine frenzy' of the poet. The more closely his work is examined, the more clearly it appears that its true nature is spasmodic and fragmentary, that Pope in reality is, *par excellence*, a writer of purple passages—a genius, that is to say, who worked according to the caprice of inspiration, by fits and starts. This fact is concealed, not contradicted, by the elaborate and amazing art with which he constructed transitions, smoothed down excrescences, and gave to the whole surface of his writing a uniform texture of brilliance and grace. What might have been inferred from internal evidence alone is substantiated by some curious particulars which have come down to us as to his habits of work. We know that constantly, during his sleepless nights, Pope was seized with an uncontrollable desire for writing. He would wake his servant, have candles lighted, and commit to paper his seething inspiration. Sometimes this would happen four times in the course of a single night. One can imagine the poet, shaken with excitement, dashing down, in the flickering candle-light, his hurried phrases. One can imagine, too, the annoyance and the perplexity of the servant; what was there in the little gentleman's writing that called for all that fuss? For us, however, the matter is clear enough. The unwitting servant was attending at the birth of immortalities—the blasting of Atossa, the crucifixion of Atticus, the rending of Sporus, or the grand *finale* of the 'Dunciad'.

Another erroneous opinion may be briefly noticed. It is too commonly held not only that Pope's matter is frigid and unemotional, but that his manner is monotonous and dull. It is unfortunate that 'George Paston' has hardly done more than touch upon this, the technical side of Pope's work, and perhaps the most important side of all. Pope himself said that his first care in writing poetry was for the sound—a statement which may well seem puzzling to those of his readers who can find nothing in his couplets but a mechanical jingle of syllables, a lifeless 'correctness' from which all the beauty and variety of true poetry have fled. But the indictment of 'correctness', originated by Warton, and crystallized by Macaulay in his essay on Byron, is in truth fallacious. Pope did not, as Macaulay supposes, strive to be 'correct' because he believed that no poetry could be good unless it obeyed a certain set of arbitrary rules. He was not a theorist, but an artist; he was not concerned with good poetry in general, but with the particular kind of poetry which he felt himself fitted to produce. That kind depended for its very existence upon the observance of strict conventions; like the architecture of Palladio and the music of Haydn, it was, by its very nature, a conventional form of art. Thus it must either be 'correct' or nothing. But an exact, regular, and ordered treatment of the heroic couplet no more implies mechanical monotony than the rigid form of a fugue. Within the limits of the convention there is an infinite scope for subtle and dexterous handling, for those fine shades and delicate gradations of sound and expression of which the secret is only known to the true artist; and it is precisely here that Pope is supreme. Impatient readers fail to observe under the surface of his 'correctness' the marvellous command of all the resources of his instrument which he in reality displays. Instances crowd his pages; but a single contrast will perhaps illustrate the range and height of his powers as clearly as any more elaborate citations. Pope is not usually thought of as a landscapist in verse; yet when he wished he could conjure up in a few words visions of rare intensity and exquisite beauty. The following couplet from the 'Dunciad' was, he declared, that which best satisfied him in the whole of his works:

'Lo! Where Moeotis sleeps, and hardly flows
The frozen Tanais through a waste of snows.'

What a picture of vast and shivering desolation ! But let us turn to another couplet in the same poem—a couplet which, as orderly, as 'smooth', as 'correct', as the other, yet produces, by the same means of subtle vowels and delicately weighted stress, an impression extraordinarily different :

> 'And happy convents, bosomed deep in vines,
> Where slumber abbots, purple as their wines.'

The verse might have been written by Keats or Tennyson. Who can be surprised that Pope said he cared for sound more than anything else?

November 20, 1909

The Poetry of Thomson*

MOST readers will probably be of opinion that Messrs
Macmillan have been a little over-generous in allowing to
James Thomson, the author of 'The Seasons', a place in
their well-known series of representative 'English Men of
Letters'. Thomson was certainly not a great poet; the
work by which he most deserves to be remembered is
slight both in bulk and quality; and his influence upon
literature, though at one time it was of considerable
importance, is now dead beyond any hope of resurrection.
Nor is there anything worthy of particular record in the
history of his life, which passed, without incident and
without romance, in easy independence among congenial
friends and patrons. It can hardly be doubted that a
concise writer could say all that need be said upon the
subject of Thomson in a magazine article of a dozen pages.
Mr Macaulay, who has succeeded in filling more than
two hundred and fifty pages, has clearly felt the difficulties
of his task. It is saying a great deal to say that in these
uncongenial circumstances Mr Macaulay is not diffuse;
but it cannot be said that he is not dull. The method which
he has adopted—that of copious paraphrase interspersed
with copious quotation—is certainly not a happy one. To
the average reader of the present day 'The Seasons', as a
whole, is an intolerably tedious piece of work; and the
tedium is by no means lessened by Mr Macaulay's device
of converting Thomson's heaviest verses into his own
equally heavy prose. Mr Macaulay belongs to the scholas-
tic school of critics. He is always careful, laborious, and

*James Thomson by G. C. Macaulay. London: Macmillan & Co.

accurate; but he is never very illuminating, nor very profound. He is at pains to inform us that the subject of his essay was above the middle height, that his wigs were unusually large, and that he was of an open, generous disposition; but, somehow or another, he has failed to bring before our minds any convincing vision of the good-natured, easygoing, comfortable 'Jemmy Thomson', who could carry his bottle with the best of them, who when his watch was stolen merely observed: 'Pshaw, I am glad they took it from me, it was never good for anything,' and who, though he lived at Richmond, never quarrelled with Pope. Similarly, with regard to Thomson's poetry, Mr Macaulay can write learnedly about diction and metre, but the essential qualities of the work which he dissects so patiently seem to elude his grasp. He is at his best when he is discussing those parts of his subject which are historical rather than literary. Thus his chapter on 'Thomson and the Poetry of Nature', in which he points out that 'The Seasons' was only the most conspicuous example of a widespread reaction against the narrow town-poetry of Pope and his school, is the most interesting in the book. But the fact that Thomson headed this reaction by no means implies that he was a 'romantic', or that he forestalled the great revolution in poetry effected by Wordsworth at the end of the eighteenth century. As Mr Macaulay observes, the most striking characteristic of Wordsworth's treatment of Nature—its intense subjectivity—is entirely absent from Thomson's verse. And there is another distinction, which so far as Thomson is concerned is more important still, for it affords the clue to an understanding of one of the chief defects of his work. Wordsworth describes Nature in the particular and in the concrete, while Thomson's descriptions are nearly always vague generalizations. Mr Macaulay alludes to Thomson's habit of 'presenting his scene in masses and in a generalized form', but he seems to regard as a merit what was undoubtedly a fatal and fundamental fault. 'The Seasons' is a descriptive poem or it is nothing; it is concerned with material objects, and it sets out to represent these objects before the reader's 'inward eye'. But what visions does it succeed in calling up? What, actually, are the scenes which it describes? It is easy to think of a hundred distinct and unforgettable pictures evoked by the poetry of Wordsworth: the daffodils dancing in their thousands, the huge peak rising over the lake in the twilight 'with measured motion, like a living thing', the vast sunset pageant witnessed by the Solitary—the list is inexhaustible; but the descriptions of Thomson leave nothing behind them upon the reader's mind. And the reason is obvious enough: they are descriptions of everything in general and nothing in particular. The account of the storm in 'Winter' begins thus:

> 'Then comes the father of the tempest forth,
> Wrapt in black glooms. First joyless rains obscure
> Drive through the mingling skies with vapour foul;
> Dash on the mountain's brow, and shake the woods,
> That grumbling wave below. The unsightly plain
> Lies a brown deluge.'

Here are rains and skies and woods, a mountain and a plain, whose only characteristic are those which are common to their kind. The rains are joyless, the skies mingle, the woods grumble, the plain is unsightly, the mountain has a brow—and that is all that we know about them; the only images that they raise are as uninteresting as they are vague. A little later we hear of 'the roused-up river', 'the rude mountain', and 'the mossy wild'; and when we inquire where the river flows, whether this mountain is identical with the last, and whether the plain and the wild are the same or different, we receive no answer. Thomson's trick of employing the definite article so as to produce the most indefinite effects is highly characteristic of his descriptive method. He is constantly telling us about 'the ruffled lake', 'the darkening forest', 'the tapering spire' and 'the conscious swain'. One longs to ask 'Which?' But it is clear that Thomson rarely had anything definite before his mind. He was not interested by the individual, the peculiar, the secret, and the unmitigated aspects of things; he was content to worship natural objects comfortably from his villa in Richmond, and the account which he gives of them is precisely what might have been expected from an intelligent gentleman who had spent his life in the suburbs.

There can be no doubt that words interested Thomson far more than things, and that fundamentally he was not a landscape painter but a rhetorician. Nature appealed to him chiefly as an excuse for fine writing. Nor would there have been any reason to object to this if his writing had been really fine. Unfortunately he was not a Milton nor a Virgil, nor even a Tennyson; he had very little taste, and he was quite without that supreme command over the magic of sound which, in a poet, will excuse not only weakness of observation, but weakness of thought. 'The Seasons' is an excellent example of what is meant by good verse as distinguished from poetry. Modelling himself upon Milton, Thomson succeeded in producing a work which bears as much resemblance to *Paradise Lost* as the hexameters of a clever sixth-form boy bear to the Georgics. He mimicked the Miltonic manner without possessing either the splendour of thought or the exaltation of spirit which, with Milton, inform and justify it. A single example will suffice to show the kind of depths into which even a clever writer like Thomson is capable of sinking when he sets out to write poetry by rule-of-thumb. Milton describes how Satan, wounded by Michael,

'Writhed him to and fro convolved.'

Thomson treasured up the Latin word, and brought it

forth on what he doubtless believed was an appropriate occasion. 'The sportive lambs,' he says,

'This way and that convolved, in friskful glee
Their frolics play.'

Such were the beauties which delighted Thomson's contemporaries and successors, and brought his writings into enormous vogue. The taste of every age has, to use Sainte-Beuve's expression, its *écueil particulier*, and the empty generalizations and academic pomposity of 'The Seasons' exactly fell in with the weak side of the taste of the eighteenth century. Perhaps the present age would have reason to be thankful if its own errors in taste were no worse than these.

Unfortunately, though 'The Seasons' is no longer a popular work, it is a famous one, and its fame has done a great deal to obscure the real merits of the poem by which Thomson does, after all, deserve to be remembered —'The Castle of Indolence'. In his treatment of this work Mr Macaulay is most disappointing. The first duty of the critic is to point out to his readers what is best worth reading in an author, and Mr Macaulay has missed an opportunity of doing a true service to lovers of literature by laying proper emphasis upon a poem which is certainly not sufficiently known. He seems hardly to have realized clearly enough that it is not quantity, nor reputation, nor historical association that gives its place to a work of art, but quality alone. 'The Seasons' is longer and more famous than 'The Castle of Indolence'. But it is not so good a poem. Mr Macaulay is unwilling to admit this; he complains that 'The Castle of Indolence' lacks unity, that its *dénouement* is unsatisfactory, and that it draws too obvious a moral. But, after all, these are points of minor importance; the essential fact about the poem is that it possesses beauty, and beauty of a rare and charming kind. Thomson in this instance was as fortunate in his model as he was unfortunate in the case of 'The Seasons'. His imitation of Spenser is graceful, easy, and, above all, light; here he is no longer a solemn dwarf strutting in a giant's robe; he wears his fancy dress with the distinction and the gaiety of a man of breeding. In spite of that lack of formal unity of which Mr Macaulay complains, he has managed to throw over the poem an imaginative atmosphere which produces a unity of its own—an atmosphere of charming languor and beautiful repose. Some of the phrases in it are not unworthy, in their exquisite felicity, to take rank with the early work of Keats. The nymph who

> 'Sighing yields her up to love's delicious harms'

must surely, by some magic of the Muses, have strayed into 'The Castle of Indolence' from the unwritten pages of 'Endymion'. And might not these lines have almost found a place in 'The Eve of St Agnes'?—

> 'While o'er his eyes the drowsy liquor ran,
> Through which his half-waked soul would faintly peep.'

Thomson sings here more feelingly of Nature's beauties than anywhere in 'The Seasons':

> 'I care not, Fortune, what you me deny:
> You cannot rob me of free Nature's grace;
> You cannot shut the windows of the sky,
> Through which Aurora shows her brightening face;
> You cannot bar my constant feet to trace
> The woods and lawns, by living stream, at eve.'

And, for sheer melody, there is nothing in the longer work which will compare with these beautiful verses:

> 'Aerial music in the warbling wind,
> At distance rising oft, by small degrees,
> Nearer and nearer came, till o'er the trees
> It hung, and breathed such soul-dissolving airs
> As did, alas! with soft perdition please:

Entangled deep in its enchanting snares,
The listening heart forgot all duties and all cares.'

But it would be easy to fill several columns with one's favourite passages in 'The Castle of Indolence'. Lovers of poetry, it may be hoped, who are unacquainted with the work may be induced by these samples to do what is always better worth doing than reading *about* a poem—read the poem itself.

March 14, 1908

The Grandiloquence of Wordsworth*

IT IS one of the functions of a great writer to destroy cut-and-dried precedents, and to give the lie to *a priori* theorizings upon the art of literature. How easy it would be to construct a complete and perfect code of the laws of poetry, if it were not for the poets! If Racine had never written *Phèdre*, for instance, who would have ventured to deny that great tragedy and the rhyming couplet are, by their very nature, incompatible? What metrical system might not be shattered by quotations from the inspired ravings of William Blake? Indeed, it would hardly be going too far to say that the surest test of the eminence of a poet is to be found in the number and the variety of the literary dogmas which he sets at naught. Shakespeare, supreme in everything, was a supreme rebel too: no rule was ever imagined which he has not triumphantly broken. From this point of view, the poetry of Wordsworth is peculiarly interesting, for Wordsworth was one of the greatest of innovators. He was the first poet who fully recognized and deliberately practised the beauties of extreme simplicity; and this achievement constitutes his most obvious title to fame. The magnitude of the revolution which he effected, the strength and the folly of the hidebound traditions which he destroyed—these facts can only be thoroughly appreciated after one has explored the forgotten versifiers of the close of the eighteenth century, and studied the mingled ridicule and abuse to which his

The Poems of William Wordsworth. Edited, with an Introduction and Notes, by Nowell Charles Smith, M.A. 3 vols. London: Methuen and Co.

early work was subjected in the reviews of the time. The
very completeness of his ultimate success has obscured the
originality of his genius, though the genius itself will
never be obscured so long as the English language lasts.
Thus, while few realize how new and strange a thing
simplicity was when Wordsworth began to write, everyone
realizes the beauty of his simplicity. Passage after passage
from his poetry filled with this quality has become part of
the common heritage of our thoughts and feelings; his
speech, so plain, so sober, and yet so exquisitely felicitous,
comes to us charged with mystery and delight, just as—to
quote a famous example of this very characteristic of his
style—

> 'The meanest flower that blows can give
> Thoughts that do often lie too deep for tears.'

Yet, curiously enough, the more one reads Wordsworth,
the more conscious one becomes of another element in his
poetry which is altogether distinct from, and even opposed
to, the kind of beauty which is most commonly associated
with his name. One sees more and more clearly that
Wordsworth was a master, not only of pure and simple
English, but of that highly coloured and splendid phraseo-
logy which, with its ornate and Latinized vocabulary, fills
the lines of so many of our greatest poets, and can hardly
be better described than by the single word 'grandiloquence'. This is borne in upon the reader all the more
forcibly when he examines Wordsworth, not in single
poems or books of selections, but, as it were, *en bloc*—when
he takes such an opportunity as is presented by Mr Nowell
Smith's new and complete edition, and ranges through the
whole mass of Wordsworth's work, from the earliest poems
to the last. Here, in Mr Smith's edition, three wonderfully
light and pleasant volumes present us with everything that
Wordsworth wrote in verse, accompanied by an excellent
introduction, and such notes as serve to illuminate, without

embarrassing, the text. And wherever we look we find, side by side with the traces of Wordsworth's severity and plainness, the no less unmistakable traces of his love of splendour and elaboration:

> 'Perhaps some dungeon hears thee groan,
>   Maimed, mangled, by inhuman men;
> Or thou upon a desert thrown
>   Inheritest the lion's den;
> Or hast been summoned to the deep,
> Thou, thou, and all thy mates, to keep
> An incommunicable sleep.'

What a sense of awful remoteness and mysterious fatality is conjured up by the long, ambiguous, Latinized words: 'inheritest', and 'summoned', and 'incommunicable'! And what little resemblance such language as this bears to that of 'conversation in the middle and lower classes of society', which, according to Wordsworth himself, it was one of his aims to reproduce! Indeed, in spite of the dogmatic assertions in his famous preface to the *Lyrical Ballads*, it is clear enough that no one was less willing than Wordsworth to be bound by his own theories. Like the seraph Abdiel in *Paradise Lost*, he was a double rebel—first against the poetical traditions of his age, and then against the doctrines which he himself had set up against them. Nor did he make any very serious pretension to consistency. It is on record that Archdeacon Hare, in conversation with him, declared on one occasion, with all the exaggerated fervour of a disciple, that the aim of a poet ought to be to use only Anglo-Saxon words, and that these, if possible, should be words of one syllable, giving as an example Wordsworth's own line: 'The world is too much with us, late and soon.' In answer, Wordsworth simply quoted from *Macbeth*: 'The multitudinous seas incarnadine', and Hare was silenced. No doubt it was obvious to Wordsworth that in poetry, if nowhere else, the end justifies the means, and

that some effects and some suggestions can only be
obtained by the use of an elaborate diction, with its freight
of reminiscences and traditional beauty. He might have
said with Dryden: 'I trade both with the living and the
dead for the enrichment of our tongue.' When his object
was the expression of simple thoughts and feelings, or the
narration of straightforward facts, he could employ
ordinary words of plain significance with the most amazing
force and skill:

> 'All, all is silent—rocks and woods,
> All still and silent—far and near!
> Only the Ass, with motion dull,
> Upon the pivot of his skull
> Turns round his long left ear.'

Nothing could be more vivid and more absolutely matter-
of-fact. But let us turn to the description of the sunrise in
the 'Excursion'—a passage too long to quote in its entirety
—and what a contrast we find!—

> 'The appearance, instantaneously disclosed,
> Was of a mighty city—boldly say
> A wilderness of building, sinking far
> And self-withdrawn into a boundless depth,
> Far sinking into splendour—without end!
> Fabric it seemed of diamond and of gold,
> With alabaster domes, and silver spires,
> And blazing terrace upon terrace, high
> Uplifted; here, serene pavilions bright,
> In avenues disposed; there, towers begirt
> With battlements that on their restless fronts
> Bore stars—illumination of all gems!
>   .   .   .   .
> Oh, 'twas an unimaginable sight!
> Clouds, mists, streams, watery rocks and emerald turf,
> Clouds of all tincture, rocks and sapphire sky,
> Confused, commingled, mutually inflamed,
> Molten together, and composing thus,

> Each lost in each, that marvellous array
> Of temple, palace, citadel, and huge
> Fantastic pomp of structure without name,
> In fleecy folds voluminous, enwrapped.'

Who can doubt that the vague and vast sublimity of this wonderful description depends upon the Latinized vocabulary? Take that away, replace the high-sounding polysyllables by their Anglo-Saxon equivalents, and you would 'leave not a wrack behind'.

Nor was it only for the sake of grandeur that Wordsworth made use of that 'poetic diction' which he had so often attacked. As his quotation from *Macbeth* shows, he was well aware of the remarkable and beautiful effects of contrast which can be produced by the close juxtaposition of Anglo-Saxon words with those of Latin origin. The 'incommunicable sleep' quoted above is an instance of this, and many others might be mentioned: 'my apprehensions come in crowds'; 'the unimaginable touch of time';

> 'The holy time is quiet as a Nun
> Breathless with adoration.'

And in perhaps the most perfect of all his poems—the eight-lined lyric beginning 'A slumber did my spirit seal'—the same effect may be noticed:

> 'No motion has she now, no force;
>   She neither hears nor sees;
> Rolled round in earth's diurnal course,
>   With rocks, and stones, and trees.'

Here the word 'diurnal', placed with consummate art among the simple Saxon monosyllables, gives a sense of colour and mystery to the whole poem which surely could have been obtained by no other means. It is remarkable that Wordsworth's love of rhetoric shows itself nowhere more often than in his sonnets. The sonnet form, 'crowding into narrow room', as he himself said, 'more of the combined effect of rhyme and blank verse than can be done by any other kind of verse I know of,' seems to demand in an especial measure a sustained pomp and concentration of language. Everyone will remember numberless lines in the sonnets where these qualities blaze and glow like the strange inward light of jewels. 'Once did she hold the gorgeous East in fee'—was there ever a more magnificent first line? And who that has once read them could ever forget the marvellous imaginative music of these words: 'Armoury of the invincible knights of old'? There seems, indeed, some reason to suppose that it was not until he had begun his study of the sonnet that Wordsworth fully realized the virtues of ornate diction. It was in May, 1802, that his first sonnets were written, after hearing his sister Dorothy read those of Milton aloud. Before that date examples of the deliberate use of Latinized language are rare in his poetry. After it they are frequent. He seems to have fallen suddenly under the influence of Milton, and his poem on the yew-trees (written in 1803) contains lines which read almost like a parody of *Paradise Lost*:

> 'Huge trunks! and each particular trunk a growth
> Of intertwisted fibres serpentine
> Up-coiling, and inveterately convolved;
> Nor uninformed with Phantasy, and looks
> That threaten the profane.'

This is an echo of the grandiloquence of Milton; but Wordsworth was never an echo—even of the greatest—for long; and the poem ends as none but he could have ended it, with a splendour and an enchantment which are all his own:

> 'In mute repose
> To lie, and listen to the mountain flood
> Murmuring from Glaramara's inmost caves.'

May 9, 1908

Coleridge's 'Biographia Literaria'*

A NEW annotated edition of Coleridge's *Biographia Literaria* has long been wanted. The charming Aldine Edition of sixty years ago with the notes and elucidations of his daughter and son-in-law is out of print and, to a large extent, out of date; and the subsequent editions have added nothing material in the way of commentary. Mr Shawcross now prints the original text with a valuable introduction and a quantity of notes, and he adds some interesting and little-known essays by Coleridge on the principles of aesthetics. His introduction, dealing particularly with the more metaphysical side of Coleridge's critical theory, is an excellent piece of work, and affords a real aid towards an understanding of the text. The only fault to be found with Mr Shawcross's commentary is that it is apt to take Coleridge a little too seriously. The *Biographia Literaria*—there is no getting over the fact—is not remarkable either for the clarity or for the cohesion of its arguments, and to impute to it the importance of a profound philosophical treatise is to divert the reader's attention from the really admirable qualities of the book. The truth is that Coleridge, in spite of—one is almost tempted to say in consequence of—his love of philosophy, was not a philosopher. He speculated too much and thought too little. His mind was constitutionally incapable of the hard and continued effort, the scrupulous precision, the systematic method, without which no reasoning, however brilliant, can be of enduring value. His temperament,

*Biographia Literaria by S. T. Coleridge. Edited, with his Aesthetical Essays, by J. Shawcross. 2 vols. Oxford: at the Clarendon Press.

as he himself confessed, was 'reverie-ish and streamy'; it was not in his nature to fight his way step by step to a definite conclusion; he wandered amiably and vaguely along the line of least resistance, and a conclusion was the last thing that he ever wished to come to. His famous theory of the imagination and the fancy, which forms the philosophical nucleus of the *Biographia Literaria*, hardly deserves the elaborate consideration which Mr Shawcross has devoted to it in his introduction. It is one of those theories which are more interesting to invent than to discuss; and in fact, when it comes to the point, Coleridge, with characteristic nonchalance, simply abandons all attempt to prove his contentions, breaking off at the very climax of the argument with a row of stars, followed by a 'letter from a friend', in consequence of which, he says, 'I shall content myself for the present with stating the main result of the chapter, which I have reserved for that future publication, a detailed prospectus of which the reader will find at the close of the second volume.' Needless to say, the 'friend' who intervened so luckily at the critical moment was Coleridge himself, and the 'letter' had been written, as he afterwards admitted, 'without taking my pen off the paper'. Devices of this kind would not have been resorted to by a serious thinker anxious to convince his readers of the truth of his opinions; but they are excusable enough in a loose, discursive essay aiming at nothing higher than suggestiveness and entertainment.

This, in fact, is the true nature of the *Biographia Literaria*. Its excellence lies in the variety of interesting subjects with which it deals, in the mass of curious information it contains, in the acuteness and originality so abundantly scattered over its pages. It gives to the reader, even more than the *Table Talk* itself, a conception of Coleridge's conversation. The *Table Talk* is a collection of unstrung gems, of thoughts detached from their context and separately set; but the essential feature of Coleridge's talk was its continuity. It was 'reverie-ish and streamy' to an extraordinary degree, and so is the *Biographia Literaria*. The fluid prose, wandering so easily and so vaguely from topic to topic, from theory to theory, from schoolboy reminiscences to an inquiry into the 'supposed irritability of men of genius', from considerations upon 'Mr Southey's works and character' to a history of the 'law of association from Aristotle to Hartley,' the anecdotes, the exhortations, the metaphysics, the endless digressions that lead nowhere in particular, and the elaborate preparations that come to nothing—all these things call up before the mind the image of Coleridge himself, shuffling along in the neighbourhood of Highgate 'at his alderman-after-dinner pace', as Keats called it, and pouring out to an amazed and silent companion his wonderful interminable talk. 'I heard his voice as he came towards me,' wrote Keats after meeting him, 'I heard it as he moved away—I heard it all the interval—if it may be called so.' This is precisely the impression which the *Biographia Literaria* gives—it makes us hear the sound of Coleridge's voice. And, it must be confessed, there are moments when the sound grows a little tiresome. These moments are generally those in which Coleridge becomes metaphysical, and begins to explain his system of aesthetics in the language of German philosophy. Nothing that Mr Shawcross can say will convince us that statements such as the following deserve very serious attention :

'Therefore, since the spirit is not originally an object, and as the subject exists in antithesis to an object, the spirit cannot originally be finite. But neither can it be a subject without becoming an object, and, as it is originally the identity of both, it can be conceived neither as infinite nor finite exclusively, but as the most original union of both. In the existence, in the reconciling, and the recurrence of this contradiction consists the process and mystery of production and life.'

Who can fail to be reminded of Carlyle's cruel account, in

his *Life of Sterling*, of the sage of Highgate, with his endlessly recurrent nasal whine about 'sum-m-ject' and 'om-m-ject'? But the reader's case is more fortunate than the listener's, for, whenever he finds that his interest is waning, he has only to turn over a page or two and start afresh. And in the present book there is assuredly no lack of engaging matter. Apart from the admirable literary criticism which abounds in it, every reader will remember with delight the humour and verve of the autobiographical sketches. Nothing could be better told than the story of Coleridge's early experiences as a journalistic bagman, and the account of the Government spy at Nether Stowey is full of excellent comedy. Wordsworth and Coleridge, sitting out all day by the seashore discussing poetry and Spinoza, had raised the suspicions of the authorities, who at that time smelt Jacobinism on every hand, and—if we are to believe Coleridge's story—a spy had actually been set upon them. The man had crept up behind a bank, and listened to their talk for hours together. 'At first he fancied that we were aware of our danger,' Coleridge says, 'for he often heard me talk of one *Spy Nozy*, which he was inclined to interpret of himself, and of a remarkable feature belonging to him; but he was speedily convinced that it was the name of a man who had made a book and lived long ago.' Perhaps the story is a little too good to be true— there is a suspicious Dogberry-and-Verges air about it; but what does that matter?

Without doubt the most interesting part of the book is that devoted to a discussion of the poetry and the literary principles of Wordsworth. Here Coleridge is in his proper element, and his examination of the poetical tenets expressed in Wordsworth's preface to the *Lyrical Ballads* is masterly and convincing. He refutes with great sagacity and an abundance of apposite illustration the paradox into which Wordsworth had been hurried by his reaction against the artificialities of the school of Pope—that the true language of poetry is the language of common speech. The vagueness and the fallaciousness of this theory meet with no mercy from Coleridge, who points out with great effect that some of the finest passages in Wordsworth's own work flagrantly contradict the rule proposed. Coleridge's criticism, however, is valuable only when he is attacking the general principles underlying Wordsworth's views; for when he begins to discuss in detail his friend's actual achievements, he shows a curious lack of sympathy and discrimination. He seems not to have perceived that Wordsworth's preface gave utterance, though in an exaggerated form, to a really important truth, which had never been recognized before in the whole history of letters—the immense aesthetic value possessed by extreme simplicity. Wordsworth, with the enthusiasm of a discoverer, overstated his case; but no overstatement could alter the fact that he had brought into the consciousness of mankind a new form of beauty. Coleridge failed to realize this; he attempted to estimate Wordsworth according to the old standards, and the result was disaster. He complained of the beautiful closing couplet in the 'Daffodils'; he complained of a fine stanza in 'Resolution and Independence'; and, unfortunately, Wordsworth listened to his complaints. All the alterations which he made in consequence of Coleridge's criticisms were undoubtedly alterations for the worse. It is a singular fact, but these chapters in the *Biographia Literaria* prove it to be certainly true—the author of 'The Ancient Mariner' was no fit judge of the 'Poems of the Imagination'.

March 7, 1908

Macaulay's Marginalia*

THIS interesting little volume contains a selection from the manuscript notes inscribed by Lord Macaulay—'in immense profusion', as his nephew tells us—on the margins of his books. Sir George Trevelyan, to whom we are indebted for the selection, adds a running commentary of his own, in which he provides such explanations as are necessary for the comprehension of the notes. Lovers of Macaulay will certainly be disappointed if they hope to find here any unexpected revelations, any new and surprising lights on the great historian's mind. There is no intercourse more private than that between a man and his books; one's midnight pencil-jottings on the margins of a favourite author are, in their very essence, confidential; if one has secrets, one tells them then. But Macaulay had no secrets. His marginalia lack the pungent quality of Swift's —where one catches a glimpse of the great splenetic Dean without, as it were, his wig and gown; nor are they marked by the sudden careless genius which inspired some of the excited scribblings of Lamb. Macaulay wrote notes in his folio Plato in exactly the same spirit as that in which he wrote an article for the *Edinburgh Review*. 'The Gorgias is certainly a very fine work. It is deformed by a prodigious quantity of sophistry. But the characters are so happily supported, the conversations so animated and natural, the close so eloquent, and the doctrines inculcated, though over-strained, are so lofty and pure, that it is impossible not to consider it as one of the greatest performances which

Marginal Notes by Lord Macaulay. Selected and Arranged by the Right Hon. Sir George Otto Trevelyan, Bart. London: Longmans and Co.

have descended to us from that wonderful generation.'
The passage might have come straight from the rough
draft of an unpublished essay; and it is a fair specimen of
the polish and elaboration of Macaulay's marginal style.
His comments on the letters and speeches of Cicero,
forming, as Sir George Trevelyan says, 'a continuous
history of the great orator's career', are even more
suggestive of the public Press, and they are perhaps the
best things in the book. It is characteristic of Macaulay
that he wrote most easily and forcibly when (whether in
posse or in *esse*) half the world was looking over his shoulder.

As a thinker Macaulay was neither original nor profound; but he possessed a compensating gift—he had the
power of expressing the most ordinary thoughts in the
most striking ways. Platitudes are, after all, the current
coin of artists, critics, and philosophers; without them all
commerce of the mind would come to a standstill; and a
great debt is owing to those who, like Macaulay, have the
faculty of minting fresh and clean and shining platitudes
in inexhaustible abundance. Macaulay brought to the
making of a platitude more fire and zest than most writers
can summon up for their subtlest and most surprising
thoughts, with the result that there are few paradoxes so
brilliant and pleasing as his commonplaces. Thus he was
unrivalled in the art of exposing, completely and finally,
an obvious piece of folly. 'So the brilliant Sophia,' wrote
Miss Seward in one of her letters, 'has commenced
Babylonian!' 'That is to say,' Macaulay wrote in the
margin, 'she has taken a house in town.' Nothing could
be more simple or more crushing. Similarly, when
Steevens, annotating a famous speech of Antony's in
which he likens a cloud to a bear, a lion, and a mountain,
observes that 'perhaps Shakespeare received the thought
from the second book of Holland's translation of Pliny's
Natural History: "In one place there appeareth the
resemblance of a waine or a chariot; in another of a

beare," ' Macaulay's comment is perfect. 'Solemn non-sense!' he wrote. 'Had Shakespeare no eyes to see the sky with?' There is nothing more to be said. And Macaulay is no less admirable in his expressions of obvious praise. 'Cornwall,' he wrote on the margin of *King Lear*, 'is, like Albany, slightly touched, but with wonderful skill. No poet ever made such strong likenesses with so few strokes.' That is excellent; but unfortunately Macaulay was not always content with the sane and the true. He had a propensity for the emphatic which hurried him too often into unjustifiable extremes. He was not satisfied with praising a thing; he must declare it to be superior to every other thing in the world. Of the conversation between Brutus and Cassius in the first act of *Julius Caesar* he exclaims: 'These two or three pages are worth the whole French drama ten times over!' That is Macaulay's way of saying 'Very good.' When he writes at the conclusion of Lear's final apostrophe to his wicked daughters: 'Where is there anything like this in the world?' no one will be inclined to quarrel with him; but the real amount of meaning to be attached to his superlatives becomes obvious when we find him writing opposite Romeo's reception of the news of Juliet's death: 'It moves me even more than Lear's agonies.' If that was so, one would like to know what he thought of *Othello*, which, Sir George Trevelyan tells us, 'Macaulay reckoned the best play extant in any language.' But there are no notes upon *Othello*. 'It may well be,' says Sir George, 'that he had ceased reading it because he knew the whole of it by heart.' No doubt Macaulay's memory was equal to that feat; but may we not suppose that there was another reason for his silence? Even Macaulay, perhaps, had exhausted his vocabulary of admiration, and had simply nothing left to say.

November 16, 1907

Dostoievsky*

OF the three great writers who dominated Russian literature during the last half of the nineteenth century, certainly the least known in England is Dostoievsky. That he is, possibly, also the best worth knowing will surprise no one who realizes the strength and solidity of international barriers in questions of literary taste. It takes a long time, even for the most enlightened of critics, to appreciate in a foreign literature anything but those qualities which it shares in common with their own. But, in general, it is precisely in its peculiar and unfamiliar qualities that the true greatness of a foreign literature is to be found. Thus for many years Tourgénieff, a writer influenced far more than either of his great contemporaries by the literary traditions of Western Europe, was the one Russian author really appreciated by English readers. Then the giant figure of Tolstoy loomed up, and it gradually came to be realized that in him lay a force of far greater potency and far greater significance. At the present moment Tolstoy undoubtedly stands with the English public for all that is most representative not only of Russian literature, but of the Russian spirit. But the English public has yet to become acquainted with Dostoievsky. This extraordinary genius, known, if at all, in England simply as the author of one work, *Crime and Punishment*, is in Russia universally recognized as at least the equal, and possibly the superior, of Tolstoy. Above all, he is acclaimed as the most distinctively *Russian* of writers;

The Brothers Karamazov by Fyodor Dostoievsky, translated into English by Constance Garnett. London: William Heinemann.

and, no doubt, it is this very fact that has so far prevented his popularity in England. There is something so strange to English readers in Dostoievsky's genius—its essence seems so unfamiliar, so singular, so unexpected—that we are naturally repelled. But having swallowed Tolstoy, there is no reason why, in time, we should not also swallow Dostoievsky. Hitherto a material difficulty has stood in the way: the English translations of Dostoievsky's work have been few, incomplete, and unsatisfactory. But with the publication by Mrs Garnett, the well-known translator of Tourgénieff and Tolstoy, of a complete and accurate translation of *The Brothers Karamazov* in a wonderfully cheap form, a great step has been made in advance. Mrs Garnett promises us the whole of the works of Dostoievsky, so that soon there should be no valid excuse for the most insular of English readers if he refrains at least from *trying* to become acquainted with a writer who, in the opinion of his countrymen, has high claims to rank as the supreme spokesman of the Russian race.

No doubt the most obviously disconcerting of Dostoievsky's characteristics is his form. Most of his works are not only exceedingly long, but—at any rate on a first inspection—extremely disordered. Even in *The Brothers Karamazov*, the last and the most carefully composed of his novels, the construction seems often to collapse entirely; there are the strangest digressions and the most curious prolixities; we have an endless dissertation, introduced apparently *à propos de bottes*, on the duties of a Russian monk; we have a long, queer story, read aloud by one of the characters in a restaurant, about Christ and a Grand Inquisitor. In some of the most important of his other works—in *The Idiot*, *The Adolescent*, and *The Possessed*—this characteristic appears in a far more marked degree. The circumstances of Dostoievsky's life certainly account in part for the looseness and incoherence of his writing. Until his closing years he was always in difficulties, always desperately in want of money, and always pouring out a flood of fiction at the highest possible pressure. Thus it was only to be expected that his composition should not have been perfect; but it seems probable that a necessity for hasty work was not the sole cause. His mind, by its very nature, did not move on the lines of judicious design and careful symmetry; it brought forth under the stress of an unbounded inspiration, and according to the laws of an imaginative vision in which the well-balanced arrangements of the ordinary creative artist held no place. Thus, the more one examines his writings and the more familiar one grows with them, the more distinctly one perceives, under the singular incoherence of their outward form, an underlying spirit dominating the most heterogeneous of their parts and giving a vital unexpected unity to the whole. The strange vast wandering conversations, the extraordinary characters rushing helter-skelter through the pages, the far-fetched immense digressions, the un-explained obscurities, the sudden, almost inconceivable incidents, the macabre humour with its extravagant exaggerations—all these things, which seem at first little more than a confused jumble of disconnected entities, gradually take shape, group themselves, and grow at last impressive and significant. The effect is like that of some gigantic Gothic cathedral, where, amid all the bewildering diversity of style and structure, a great mass of imaginative power and beauty makes itself mysteriously felt, and, with its uncertain proportions and indefinite intentions, yet seems to turn by comparison even the purest and most perfect of classical temples into something stiff and cold.

But, besides the looseness of his construction, there is another quality in Dostoievsky's work which is calculated to prove an even more serious stumbling-block to English readers. His books are strange not only in form, but in spirit. They seem to be written by a man who views life from a singular angle; everything in them is agitated, feverish, intense; they are screwed up above the normal pitch; they appear to be always trembling on the verge of insanity, and sometimes, indeed, to plunge over into the very middle of it. Now this kind of atmosphere offers a peculiarly marked contrast to that of the ordinary English novel. The great tradition of English fiction has flowed steadily—from Defoe, through Fielding, Scott, Miss Austen, Thackeray, George Eliot, right down to the present day, to George Gissing and to Mr Arnold Bennett —in a totally contrary direction. With a very few exceptions (Emily Brontë is the most outstanding of them) all our great novelists have been writers whose fundamental object has been to treat of life from the standpoint of common sense; to present it with sanity, with breadth, with humour; to throw over their vision of it the plain clear light of day, and to stand on one side themselves, with the detachment of amused and benevolent spectators. The result has been a body of literature remarkable for its sobriety, its humanity, and its quiet wisdom; and it is only natural that a reader who has grown accustomed to these qualities should be perplexed and jarred when he comes upon the extravagance and the frenzy that seethe in Dostoievsky's pages. Yet here again the difficulty, to one who refuses to be rebuffed by first impressions, will turn out to be more apparent than real. Paradoxical as it may seem, it is yet certainly true that Dostoievsky, with all his fondness for the abnormal and the extraordinary, is a profoundly sane and human writer. In this respect, indeed, he is the exact opposite of Tolstoy, who conceals a neurotic temperament under the cloak of a strict and elaborate adherence to the commonplace. Dostoievsky, while refusing to turn away his eyes from what is horrible, grotesque, and disgraceful in life, does not, like the French writers of the Naturalistic School, take a pleasure in these things, and deal out pessimism with an acrimonious relish; on the contrary, he only faces the worst in order to assert, with a

12

fuller courage and a deeper confidence, the nobility and splendour of the human spirit. He can depict, side by side with the distorted and excessive creatures who fill his canvases, figures of the rarest beauty and the most exquisite purity—Aliosha in *The Brothers Karamazov*, Muichkin in *The Idiot*, Sonia in *Crime and Punishment*. But his sympathy does not stop short with virtue and loveliness; there is something infinite in it. He can show us characters where all that is base, absurd, and contemptible is mingled together, and then, in the sudden strange vision that he gives us of their poignant underlying humanity, he can make us lay aside our scorn and our disgust, endowing us with what seems a new understanding of the mysterious soul of man. No other writer ever brought forth with a more marvellous power the 'soul of goodness in things evil'.

This power is but one manifestation of the wonderful intensity and subtlety of Dostoievsky's psychological insight. Here, no doubt, lies the central essence of his genius, the motive force which controls and animates the whole of his work. It is his revelations of the workings of the human mind that give him his place among the great creative artists of the world. But in other directions his ability is hardly less remarkable: in the unforgettable vividness of his descriptions, in his singularly original sense of humour, in his amazing capacity for crowding his stage with a multitude of persons, all interacting and all distinct, as in the famous account of the Convicts' Bath in the *House of the Dead*. One minor instance of his mastery over the resources of his art may be noticed—his extraordinary power of describing dreams. There can be no doubt that the nightmares of Dostoievsky (and there are many) throw all other attempts that have ever been made in that direction into insignificance. Perhaps an unsympathetic critic might declare that this was to be expected, since his books are all of them in reality little else than prolonged nightmares. But to how many of the highest works of man might not the same criticism be applied? To *King Lear*, for instance. And indeed, if one seeks for comparison, it is to the Elizabethan dramatists that one must turn to find kindred spirits with Dostoievsky. In his pages one finds again, as in an unexpected transmigration, the pathos, the terror, and the awful humour of Webster, the 'inspissated gloom' of Tourneur, the tragic intensity of Middleton, the morbid agonies of Ford. The same vast and potent inspiration which filled so erratically and yet so gloriously those old poets of Renaissance England still seems to breathe and burn through the novels of the modern Russian. There is more than an echo in him of Shakespeare himself. The art which wove out of the ravings of three madmen in a thunderstorm the noblest and profoundest symphony that human hearts have ever listened to is, in its essence, the same art that went to the making of *The Idiot* and *The Possessed*.

September 28, 1912

E. The Theatre

Shakespeare on the Stage

It is difficult not to sympathize with those fastidious
people—so great a critic as Charles Lamb was one of
them—who refuse to see Shakespeare acted. The in-
adequacy of any scenic apparatus in representing a
spiritual conflict, which supplied the basis for Lamb's
argument, will doubtless always remain the really crucial
objection against the public performance of imaginative
dramas; but there are other considerations which, if they
are less fundamental, appeal perhaps even more strongly
to the ordinary lover of Shakespeare. There is, for instance,
the unpleasant sense of shock produced by the violent
imposition of an alien conception of some favourite scene
in place of our own private and habitual imaginings. The
merit of the actors' presentment is of very little consequence; it is enough that they have forced upon us a
vision which is not our vision, and we turn from it with
the same sort of irritated disgust as that produced by a set
of illustrations to Scott or Miss Austen. And then there is
the inevitable vulgarization which, in every dramatic
performance, must to some extent do injury to thoughts
and expressions which have already become familiar to us
through the quiet medium of the printed page. What is
spoken to a crowd cannot, however beautifully it may be
spoken, possess quite the same charm as the silent
utterance of the poet to oneself alone. Yet, when all is said
and done, objections of this kind strike the hardened playgoer as somewhat trivial and somewhat irrelevant; it is as
if one were to complain to a foxhunter that riding was
intolerable because of the jolts. Jolts or no jolts, people, as a

matter of fact, continue to ride, and, whatever the susceptibilities of certain critics, the plays of Shakespeare continue to be acted. At the present moment, at the Lyceum and His Majesty's, *Romeo and Juliet* and *The Merchant of Venice* are being welcomed nightly by full houses. It is impossible to blink the fact that, after three hundred years, Shakespeare's drama remains a living force upon the stage. And since this is so, it can only be regretted that literary critics persist in applying their powers exclusively to the literary side of Shakespeare's work and ignore altogether its relation to the art of acting. To do this is merely to widen the breach between theory and practice, and thus to diminish still further the likelihood of a truly artistic tradition of Shakespearean acting coming into existence. As matters stand, the whole burden of the interpretation of Shakespeare falls upon the actors. They are like builders who have been given the architect's plans and then left entirely to their own devices. They do their best according to their lights, but their lights are still those of builders, and not those of architects. The literary critic, whose business it is to supervise and to instruct, has deserted them; and who can be surprised if the result is a house which, though it may roughly carry out the architect's intention, is full of details not in the highest architectural taste?

Nothing shows more clearly the extent to which the representation of Shakespeare is dominated by the views and the requirements of actors than the kind of rearrangement which his plays are made to undergo whenever they appear upon the stage. Some of these rearrangements are no doubt due to the modern system of scenery, which necessitates a greater cohesion in the action; but this is so far from being the only cause that it is no uncommon thing for actors to divide what in the original was one long scene into two. The underlying motive for the greater part of the alterations is not mechanical, but histrionic; they proceed from the craving which seems to be implanted in the breast of every actor for working up the action into a series of well-marked climaxes, each climax being followed immediately by the fall of the curtain, so that none of its effect may be lost. It is only natural that an actor should have this craving, for every such climax means an opportunity for a personal triumph, which, however obvious and spectacular it may be, still has the supreme advantage of focusing the whole attention of the audience upon himself. But it is none the less certain that crude effects of this kind find no place in Shakespeare's drama. This is partly explained by the fact that in his day the theatre was unprovided with a curtain; but it is clear enough that his whole conception of dramatic art was quite alien to the modern habit of bringing every scene to a close immediately the action has reached its height. A single instance will suffice to illustrate this. The balcony scene in *Romeo and Juliet* ends at the Lyceum on Romeo's beautiful couplet:

> 'Sleep dwell upon thine eyes, peace in thy breast!
> Would I were sleep and peace, so sweet to rest!'

But in the original text the scene does not end here. Romeo adds another couplet:

> 'Hence will I to my ghostly father's cell,
> His help to crave and my dear hap to tell.'

Perhaps Shakespeare was wrong thus to bring his hero and his audience back to the common earth, and not to end his wonderful scene on a note of lyrical rapture; but, whether he was wrong or right, it was Shakespeare's way. A more significant example of the same tendency occurs in *The Merchant of Venice*. As the play is acted at His Majesty's the curtain drops on the trial scene at Shylock's exit, and the incident of the rings follows in another scene outside the Doge's palace. Mr Tree explains in his programme his reason for the alteration. 'It has frequently been felt,' he says, 'that the incidents of the gloves and the rings, following immediately after the tragedy of Shylock, have been in something of the nature of an anticlimax.' But by whom has this 'frequently been felt'? Doubtless by actors, and principally by the particular actor who happens to take the part of Shylock. For him it is all-important that the curtain should come down with a run upon his departure from the Court; whatever follows after that must be, so far as his effect upon the audience is concerned, an 'anticlimax' indeed. But Shakespeare was not thinking of a particular actor; he was thinking of the play as a whole; and the 'anticlimax' of which Mr Tree complains completely serves the purpose of giving an impression of reality to the whole scene. The actor, to secure one of his favourite climaxes, loses an effect which is in truth far more dramatic, because it is far more real—the momentary hush after Shylock's exit, followed by the matter-of-fact talk of the dispersing Court.—'Sir, I entreat you home with me to dinner.'—Could there be a more poignant summary of the relentless indifference with which the world looks upon a tragedy, and passes on? But actors will have none of this, because, being actors, it is only natural that they should prefer what is stagy to the image of life itself.

The same sacrifice of the truly artistic and the real to the false and the over-emphatic is to be seen in what is perhaps an even more important side of the actors' treatment of Shakespeare—their delivery of his words. On the whole, the style of delivery at present in vogue could hardly be worse. It is true that the difficulties are great. Shakespeare's matter is often highly subtle and sometimes obscure; it has to be made plain to a mixed audience in a large theatre; and there is the added complication of the verse. But nothing can be more certain than that the method by which our actors try to circumvent these

difficulties is radically mistaken. Their object seems to be
to buoy up the meaning of the words they utter by all the
stage devices at their command—by exaggerated gesture
and ceaseless movement, by forced laughter and preposterous sighings and undercurrents of incidental music,
by an intolerable slowness of enunciation, and by an
intonation of the blank verse more barbarous than can be
described. These are merely the refuges of weakness, like
the attempts of a bad writer to obtain emphasis by underlinings and italic type. After all, Shakespeare can stand on
his own merit; and that actor will always produce the
greatest effect who can convey to his audience most
completely, not this or that contrivance for elucidating
Shakespeare's meaning, but simply and solely what
Shakespeare actually wrote. What a relief it is when for a
moment or two there is peace upon the stage, and we
begin to hear the words and to follow the thoughts of the
highest of poets and the most profound of philosophers!
But these moments are rare and brief; they are interrupted
by an expressive march across the stage, or by a burst of
explanatory music from the orchestra, and we are back
again once more among the old theatrical phantoms. Nor
is it only the sense of the words that is distorted and
obscured by this kind of treatment; the characters themselves, and the whole atmosphere of the play, undergo a
similar change. Who could recognize in the sprawling,
shouting, guffawing Mercutio at the Lyceum the airy
gentleman of Shakespeare's fancy, or in the Portia at His
Majesty's, with her affected grandeur, her barefaced
sentimentality, and her laborious giggles, the lady whom
we love? Why is it that while in modern plays ladies and
gentlemen are acted as ladies and gentlemen, in plays by
Shakespeare they must be acted as minxes and buffoons?
There seems to be a convention upon the stage that what
is 'Shakespeare' cannot be natural, that it is too great for
common usage, that it must be propped up and decorated

and explained. But the convention contradicts itself. If Shakespeare is truly great, he needs no trickery. When will our theatres begin to recognize this simple fact? Until they do, we must be prepared to face the absurd anomaly of the greatest dramatist in the world being acted as if he were the worst.

April 25, 1908

Mr Hawtrey

THE English playgoer who has an evening on his hands, and who wishes to run no risks in his search for entertainment, can always make sure of satisfaction by the simple plan of going to see Mr Hawtrey. Other actors may provide a more elaborate, a more highly seasoned, or a more *recherché* fare, but none can be relied upon with quite the same kind of certainty. With Mr Hawtrey alone one is absolutely safe from any danger of being bored, or teased, or disgusted; his dishes are simple, unassuming, unvarying, and always perfectly cooked. Yet it is true that what Mr Hawtrey has to offer, though it certainly cannot be called exotic, is possessed of a flavour of its own which is quite unmistakable. This flavour is difficult to analyse; but whatever else might be said about it, one of its characteristics is obvious enough—it is peculiarly English; indeed, it is hard to think of anything more completely and typically English than Mr Hawtrey's acting. For this reason, no doubt, our foreign visitors are apt to be puzzled by his success. To them he is, of all our institutions—and surely he deserves to be described as an institution—perhaps the most mysterious. When they have understood our hansoms, our cooking, and our table of precedence, they are still baffled by Mr Hawtrey. 'You English,' exclaimed a French acquaintance, 'are so paradoxical that your favourite actors are those that never act. What other people would put themselves to the trouble and expense of going to a theatre in order to see a gentleman appear upon the stage, and behave there precisely as a gentleman always does behave, neither more nor less? You do this, and you are not content with doing it once; you do it night after night, month after month, and year after year. You are never happier than when you are watching, for the thousandth time, the same behaviour and the same gentleman.' Certainly, on the face of the matter, there is much to be said for our neighbour's point of view. Compared with the vast range of a Coquelin or the exquisite variety of a Bartet, Mr Hawtrey's achievement must strike everyone as somewhat meagre and somewhat monotonous. He works along a single line, so to speak, and that line is the line of least resistance. He prefers to do one thing very well an indefinite number of times rather than to branch off into new experiments and snatch adventurous successes. And for this it is clear that his audiences are in great part responsible. 'It was alway yet the trick of our English nation,' says Falstaff, 'if they have a good thing, to make it too common.' The words are singularly true at the present day, when the endeavours of our artists in every field of production are hampered and stultified by the public demand for repetition. A painter who makes a hit with a picture of scaffolding finds himself in danger of being obliged to paint nothing but scaffolding for the rest of his life; and instances of the same kind are unhappily frequent upon the stage. Mr Hawtrey, however, escapes the worst evils of this system, because it so happens that in his case the part which the public insists upon his playing is, there can be very little doubt, the part which actually suits him best. It is, of course, impossible to make quite sure of this; for anything we know to the contrary, there may lie concealed in Mr Hawtrey a fund of un-explored capabilities; he may have within him the makings of a supremely melodramatic villain, or a dazzling hero of romance. How pleasant it would be if we could make a few experiments—if, by some magic or some persuasion, we could induce Mr Hawtrey to appear before us as Shylock, let us say, or Hamlet, or Tony Lumpkin, or 'Enery Straker! That would be truly interesting; but unfortunately our curiosity on such points as these is never likely to be satisfied. All that we shall ever know for certain is that Mr Hawtrey is admirable as he is; and perhaps on the whole it is wiser to enjoy the good things we have than long for others that we know not of.

But Mr Hawtrey's popularity suggests another weakness on the part of English audiences, the existence of which it is impossible to deny, and which is more serious than the desire to 'make a good thing too common'. The essence of Mr Hawtrey's acting lies in its immaculate gentility; there is its central charm, its unfailing fascination. But there are two ways of enjoying the portrayal of such qualities: there is the natural and proper delight in the representation of things that are in themselves admirable, and there is the very different kind of pleasure which springs from a foolish self-complacency or a vulgar worship of caste, and which is merely a subtle form of snobbery. More than any other nation, perhaps, the English appreciate what is excellent in the ideal gentleman; and for that very reason they are more prone than other nations to fall into error in their attitude towards social distinctions. In theory it is true that the difference between snobbery and a genuine love of the qualities which go to make a gentleman is immense, and yet in practice the two feelings merge into one another, and it needs a refined mind and a cultivated taste to realize exactly where the one ends and the other begins. An example of this may be seen in two of the plays in which Mr Hawtrey's success has been conspicuous—*The Man from Blankley's*, and the piece in which he is at present acting at the Vaudeville Theatre, *Jack Straw*. These plays are concerned with precisely the same theme: the fatuity and the vulgarity of the snob as opposed to the dignity and the sense of the true gentleman. In Mr Anstey's charming comedy this subject is handled with the utmost delicacy;

the whole action passes in an atmosphere of ease and laughter, and the result is a creation rare enough in dramatic literature—a social satire which is at once pointed and good-natured. Very different, however, is the treatment of the same initial idea in *Jack Straw*. Here Mr Anstey's fine contours are blurred or exaggerated; here, instead of observation, we have the obvious, instead of lightness, the grotesque. The fine gentleman is far too conscious of his own high breeding, and the snobs, over-emphasized and impossible, remind us of the fact that the most insidious form of snobbishness is that which is for ever occupied with the snobbishness of others. Nevertheless, in spite of these faults—or shall we rather say because of them?—*Jack Straw* has been, if anything, more successful than *The Man from Blankley's*. The public seems to have failed to discriminate between real taste and the imitation of taste, though doubtless this very fact may be regarded as an additional tribute to Mr Hawtrey's influence. His acting, needless to say, is always impeccable; whenever he is on the stage we forget that we are listening to what is merely second-rate; he almost persuades us to believe not only that the character which he himself impersonates is really a gentleman, but that the other characters whom he tricks and humiliates are really snobs.

For, after all, when Mr Hawtrey is concerned, the play is emphatically *not* the thing. What is the thing is simply and solely Mr Hawtrey. Thus to say that he is always himself is in reality not an impeachment of his art, but his best justification. For what we are interested in is his own character—the irresponsible, lazy, light-hearted, suscep-tible, and faintly ridiculous gentleman whom, in a curious, delightful way, across the footlights, we have come to know so well. Mr Hawtrey's art is, like all art, a method of expression; but it differs from that of the ordinary actor in that it is primarily concerned with expressing, not an alien character, but his own. Thus, from one point of view, it comes nearer to the more strictly creative arts, though unfortunately, unlike them, it is, by its very nature, transitory. Its finest manifestations cannot outlive their author. Let us enjoy them, then, while we may.

November 28, 1908

Mr Granville Barker

THE conclusion of the series of 'Vedrenne-Barker' performances at the Savoy Theatre, accompanied by Mr Barker's own withdrawal—let us hope it is only a temporary one—from the English stage, brings to a close a memorable incident in the theatrical history of the last few years. It is hardly too much to say that the companies which, under Mr Barker's leadership, drew such crowded and enthusiastic audiences to the Court and the Savoy accomplished something like a revolution in the art of dramatic production in England. Perhaps the most striking feature of Mr Barker's management was its continuity. Though his companies were not always identical, they were imbued with a single spirit, and worked for the same ends. English playgoers began to understand for the first time what a school of acting means; they began to realize that the system of stars and actor-managers is not without its drawbacks, and that the subordination of individual aims to the interests of art might be not only meritorious but successful. Mr Barker founded a tradition, and justified it by success; nor can there be any doubt that the example of his school will exercise a potent influence on the development of English acting.

But of no less importance than the establishment of such a tradition was the nature of the ideals underlying it. Mr Barker and his colleagues set out to make an appeal to a side of the average playgoer which most actors—and especially English actors—are in the habit of disregarding altogether: they appealed to his intellect. Their most successful and most characteristic productions were presentations of Mr Shaw's comedies—works in which the brilliant dialogue and the paradoxical wit are for the most part the expression of a high originality and vivacity of thought. And they were, besides, the means of introducing to the public a number of serious and thoughtful plays by new writers, such as Mr Galsworthy and Mr Barker himself. But their intellectual quality showed itself no less clearly in their style of acting than in the nature of the plays which they performed. It was here that Mr Barker's management made its most unmistakable mark. The least observant spectator felt that in the acting which flourished under Mr Barker's auspices there was a reality and a vitality which could not be found elsewhere. The stage seemed for once no longer stagy, and what passed there took on, in a surprising and delightful fashion, the complexion of actual life. For the first time the players appeared to have thoroughly understood 'the purpose of playing' as Hamlet defined it—'whose end, both at the first and now, was and is, to hold, as 'twere, the mirror up to nature; to show virtue her own feature, scorn her own image, and the very age and body of the time his form and pressure.' There can be no doubt that this result could never have been achieved without a high degree of technical skill, a remarkable capacity for collective effort, and a rare power of observation. But these qualities would have availed little without the aid of another and a more fundamental one—intellectual ability. Mr Barker tried the bold experiment of treating his audience as if it were composed of rational human beings who knew the difference between rant and eloquence, who were more interested in people than in puppets, and who had their wits about them. The majority of actors look upon an audience very much as a general looks upon an army—as a body that can only move at the speed of its slowest member. They advance with such patient emphasis, such careful underlinings of every point, and such explanatory exaggerations of every sentiment that the effect produced is curiously remote from the 'form and pressure' of the bustling time we live in. Mr Barker, it is plain, realized that these were antiquated methods, and that the one indispensable ingredient for a truly natural style of acting was quickness. His great elocutionary powers enable him, when he wishes, to make use of a delivery which is at once remarkably rapid and absolutely clear; but this, of course, is merely a subsidiary detail in his general treatment of his art. The main principle by which he is guided is, obviously enough, the Heracleitean one—that the world is a flux, a succession of delicately graduated phases which melt into one another with almost imperceptible subtlety, instead of being—as the old-fashioned actor would make it—a collection of startingly articulated 'points'. Thus, in order to 'hold, as 'twere, the mirror up to nature', it is the actor's business to practise not only a physical quickness in fluency of voice and subtlety of gesture, but a quickness of mind, an alertness and adroitness of intellect, which can pass easily from thought to thought, from emotion to emotion, which understands the art of hinting and of taking things for granted, and knows how to be expressive by skill rather than by force. This was the kind of art with which Mr Barker, assisted by a brilliant group of actors and actresses who shared his ideals, appealed to the public; and, as might have been foretold, the appeal was not made in vain. Audiences, called upon to use their wits, were delighted by the unexpected compliment; the most lethargic began to enjoy the exercise; and Mr Barker was able to set the pace.

It would, however, be very far from the truth to describe Mr Barker as an intellectual actor, and nothing more. One of the principal causes of his artistic success is that he can mingle intellect with fancy, and his acting is often at its sprightliest when it is most significant. He possesses in a high degree the indefinable quality of charm—a quality which he displays at its fullest perhaps in his rendering of Valentine in *You Never Can Tell*, and in the delightful third act of *The Doctor's Dilemma*. More than any other English actor, he can 'put a spirit of youth in everything', so that the whole scene becomes charged with airy gaiety and irresponsible high spirits. Thus he avoids the fault which besets the actor who is primarily intellectual—that of a too persistent seriousness. When he is on the stage one never feels—as one sometimes does at the Paris Théâtre Antoine, for instance—that the artistic effort is too obvious, the ingenuity too complete, and the whole effect worked out with such consummate skill as to verge on the pedantic. With Mr Barker the art and the ingenuity are there, but they are softened and etherealized by a perpetual flow of English humour and English imagination. Here he is aided by his voice, with its haunting, half-mocking intonations, and its power of suggesting unutterable things. Indeed—if we might hazard the fancy—it is in his voice that Mr Barker's spirit has its habitation. There lies the central essence of his individuality, the subtle secret of his charm. There, too, lies the gravest danger for the future of Mr Barker's art. It is no uncommon thing for an actor to become obsessed by his own personality, and to grow at last into something little better than a parody of himself. Mr Barker's voice, with its intensely personal flavour, is an instrument precisely fitted to work such a catastrophe, unless it be most jealously controlled. There have been signs in some of his later appearances that Mr Barker was beginning to be mastered by his own voice; he seemed once or twice to be speaking rather for the sake of his voice than for the sake of his part. Let us hope that these apparent affectations were nothing more than accidents, and that Mr Barker will long continue to delight us by being—what, after all, he has no need to be afraid of being—simply himself.

March 28, 1908

Coquelin

To English theatre-goers perhaps the most striking point about the performances now being given by M. Coquelin at His Majesty's is the immense variety of his rôles. During the few weeks of his stay he is to appear in a series of impersonations that covers nearly every branch and gradation of the comic spirit. Tartufe and M. Perrichon, Figaro and M. Jourdain, Cyrano de Bergerac and Mascarille: M. Coquelin passes from one to the other—and the list might be greatly extended—with consummate ease and an art which very rarely indeed fails to carry complete conviction. What a contrast this kind of versatility offers to some of our English actors, who, for so long as one can remember, have played along a single groove, endlessly repeating themselves with unwearied regularity! In many cases, no doubt, the groove is a delightful one, but for all that it is a groove. Who, for instance, has ever been surprised by Mr Hawtrey? One goes to see him, as one goes to a familiar restaurant, to get what one has always had before—the presentation of a foolish, amatory, exceedingly lazy, and wholly amusing English gentleman. And similarly we may be sure, whenever Sir Charles Wyndham appears upon the stage, of finding a sentimental, chivalrous, and middle-aged bachelor. But a stray visitor at His Majesty's could make no such prophecies. He might come upon the amiable absurdity of *Le Bourgeois Gentilhomme*, or the electric cynicism of *Figaro*, or the fantastic gaiety of *Les Précieuses Ridicules*, or the slime and the horror of *Tartufe*. Yet amid all these diversities M. Coquelin succeeds in preserving what is, after all, the actor's most potent spell—the sense of personality. Whether one is being charmed, or tickled, or terrified, one knows well enough that it is Coquelin who is, so to speak, doing the trick. It is this combination of individuality and dramatic power which forms the basis of his art. He has not allowed his own personality to get the better of his histrionic sense, but has found the way of projecting it, in all its vitality, into whatever mould may come to hand. Thus his greatest successes are, *par excellence*, successes in the representation of character. He is never intellectually profound; he never reaches the heights of passion; but he is always a human being whom we intimately know. His power of grasping the unity and the complexity of the creature whom he represents is only less admirable and amazing than the triumphant skill with which he brings his conception in all its breadth and subtlety into life upon the stage.

No one could hesitate for a moment as to the means by which M. Coquelin arrives at the most telling and the most characteristic of his effects. His face is his great instrument; it is there that the central magic of his art is to be found. Other actors convey their finest impressions through the voice, or through the expressiveness of bodily motions; with M. Coquelin these things are merely accessories, and it is hardly an exaggeration to say that if he were to put his head through a curtain and act to a deaf audience nothing of importance would be lost. It is often when he is silent and motionless that he is most triumphant. To mention a single instance, who that has once seen it can ever forget the awful, shattered visage of his Tartufe in the last speechless moment of despair? How difficult it is to believe that these are the same features which flash and quiver with the folly of Mascarille! There is something so inexhaustible in M. Coquelin's face, there is such a wealth of variety in it, such an infinite succession of subtle and shifting moods, that one is tempted to

compare it with some natural object—the sea or the sky—
wherein one may always find a new and absorbing
significance. Its fascination makes itself felt nowhere more
forcibly than in M. Sardou's new play, *L'Affaire des
Poisons*, for here there is very little interest apart from
the spectacular, and the spectacle which, among all the
rest, reigns supreme is that of M. Coquelin's face. It is
impossible to give any attention to the gorgeous dresses
and the elaborate decorations—the resuscitated pomp and
splendour of Louis XIV's Court—so long as the Abbé
Griffard, with that wonderful countenance of his, is upon
the stage. In comparison, the faces of the other actors
seem to be things cut out of wood. But M. Coquelin's
endowment is, of course, not merely physical. The natural
mobility and expressiveness of his face have been cultivated with such assiduity and such art that they have
become engines of the most exquisite delicacy, ready to
respond alike to the slightest and the most elaborate
suggestions of the mind within. In the part of the Abbé
Griffard the main interest centres round a series of
equivocating conversations, in which the sly and subtle
priest detects the devices of his enemies by assuming a
masque of countrified ingenuousness. This situation of
double innuendo is admirably calculated to exhibit the
resources of M. Coquelin's skill. He has to deceive his
interlocutor upon the stage, and he has to show the
audience that he is doing so. It is easy to imagine how
some of our own melodramatists would treat the part—the
flashing glances, the obvious asides, the struttings to and
fro, the sudden starts and the hissing ejaculations, which
serve soon enough to make the audience understand that
a trick is being played, but leave them wondering how so
obvious a fact can escape the notice of the victim.
M. Coquelin's method is altogether different. He con-
vinces us that this indeed is the very manner of successful
dissimulation, and that the cleverest villain in the world

would be taken in by such arts as those; until at last we begin to realize that, since we ourselves are not taken in, we must be looking, not at a piece of deception, but at a piece of acting, and that a thousand subtle indications of facial expression have been telling us the very secret which they seemed to hide. Nothing can be more instructive than to compare such a double-edged performance as this with the wholly contrary representation of a M. Jourdain. Here the impression produced is one of concentrated fatuity, of folly which is never for a moment conscious of its own existence; and one is left wondering whether, after all, the subtlety which can take upon itself the form of such simplicity is not more amazing than the other.

M. Coquelin is at his strongest in parts of pure comedy; he is at his weakest in parts of sentiment and romance. Thus his performance of Cyrano de Bergerac displays very few of his merits and lays bare his most obvious defects. M. Rostand's hero can only be made convincing upon one condition—that he is played with genuine spontaneity; and this is the one condition M. Coquelin cannot fulfil. Deliberation is the soul of his acting, and deliberate spontaneity is a contradiction in terms. However clever the imitation, however elaborate the workmanship, high spirits that are machine-made will always ring false. M. Coquelin has no touch of that peculiarly English quality of sudden imaginative humour possessed, for example, in such an eminent degree, by Mr James Welch. His humour is admirable from every point of view except this; it is too carefully prepared to be able to seize upon those strong places of comic art which can only be taken, as it were, by assault; and thus the wild *gasconnades* of Cyrano fall flat from M. Coquelin's lips. There is, too, a further reason why this particular play is ill-suited to this particular actor. The play has not the breath of life in it; it is in essence sentimental and melodramatic; and even its verse labours under the disadvantage of being imitative and insincere. A great romantic actor might lift it for a moment into a region which is not its own—the high region of poetry and imagination. But M. Coquelin is a great comic actor, and comedy cannot exist apart from the realities of human life. Thus his triumphs are not to be looked for in the world of dreams and sentiments, but in the world of laughter and fact—in the world of Labiche, and Beaumarchais, and Molière.

June 27, 1908

Mr Beerbohm Tree

THE performance at His Majesty's of *The Mystery of Edwin Drood* has been chiefly interesting as affording, in a compact and vivid manner, an example of Mr Beerbohm Tree's conception of the art of acting. The play, as a play, was in no way convincing or significant; it had not even that 'bad eminence' in raw emotionalism possessed by less restrained melodramas; its only merit was that it showed us Mr Tree, and nothing but Mr Tree. The attention was not distracted by those suggestions of poetry or plot or dramatic situation which—one is half ashamed to admit it—do occasionally creep into the mind during his revivals of Shakespeare, or his productions of Mr Stephen Phillips's plays; the whole of the interest was centred in the actor. And doubtless all who witnessed Mr Tree's performance of John Jasper did so, if not with thrilled excitement, at least with a pleased curiosity sufficiently active to carry them through the piece without a touch of tedium. Yet how many of those who watched the stage from the first moment to the last with absorbed attention took the same feelings away with them after the fall of the curtain? Mr Tree's acting always seems to raise, in a greater or less degree, this curious kind of contradiction. While it lasts, we are attentive, amused, and interested; when it is over, a feeling of flatness and barrenness, a feeling almost of dejection, comes over our minds. If we could account for this, we should perhaps come nearer to a true understanding of the fundamental qualities of Mr Tree's art. But in any case, it seems clear that the kind of acting which leaves upon the spectator either no permanent impression at all or an unpleasant one cannot be a really good kind; and the further question suggests itself: Why, if Mr Tree's acting is not really good, is it so eminently successful?

To all these questions there is no doubt an obvious answer, which is to a great extent the true one. Mr Tree— and with Mr Tree we are considering the whole class of actors of which he is the most prominent member— succeeds only in his treatment of detail, and fails altogether to produce a fine or convincing general effect. His acting reminds us too often of a building in the bad style of florid architecture, where the structure is obliterated and lost under the mass of irrelevant ornament. For the moment the ornament attracts, but the impression which it produces is supported and dominated by no great lines, no massive proportions, so that in the end the only effect that is left upon the mind is one of insignificant display. Mr Tree is so anxious to make 'points', and to make them as thoroughly as possible, that he constantly forgets that the first aim of the actor should be to produce an impression which is consistent and artistic as a whole. He sacrifices the lasting unity of dramatic effect to a succession of minor effects which are merely momentary. In *The Tempest*, for instance, he was sometimes a sentimental child of Nature and sometimes a ridiculous buffoon, with the inevitable result that he was never Caliban. Similarly, as Mark Antony in *Julius Caesar* he lost a great opportunity in the oration over Caesar's body owing to his inability to resist the temptation of bringing off a momentary *coup*. The whole significance of the scene depends upon the mob, which, under the spell of Antony's oratory, turns gradually from indifference to interest, from interest to sympathy, and from sympathy to rage. It is a marvellous study of crescendo in human passion, and ought, if treated adequately, to produce overwhelming effect. As Mr Tree performed it, the mob in a few moments changed violently from one extreme to the other; the sudden transition was striking, but that was all; it showed Antony, perhaps, as a greater orator than even Shakespeare had made him; but it shattered at a blow the supreme dramatic significance of Shakespeare's scene. The same tendency, though in a somewhat different form, made its appearance in *Edwin Drood*. Here Mr Tree seemed only anxious to do one thing—to suggest murder at every possible opportunity He was, without a moment's intermission, all horror, all terror, all guilt. A leaf dropped, and he clutched the air with frantic fingers; he could never speak without first looking over his shoulder, and he could never look over his shoulder without first rolling his eyes. Each lurid grimace, each dreadful attitude, held the attention; but, in the meantime, where was the character of John Jasper? It had been forgotten altogether, it had disappeared under a cloud of melodramatic 'points'. One felt, as one watched Mr Tree's perpetually gruesome figure, that John Jasper possessed all the qualities of a murderer, except one—that of being a man. So long as he was on the stage one was attracted by the successive tricks and gestures, but the attraction necessarily ceased the moment the curtain fell. Mr Tree is like a spendthrift who produces the impression of wealth by living on his capital, and who when he dies turns out to have left nothing at all.

But there is another, and a deeper, explanation of the combined fascination and fruitlessness of Mr Tree's acting. No one can have failed to observe the immense stress which he invariably lays on facial expression, on gesture, on scenic decoration, on costume, on everything, in fact, which goes to make up the outward appearances of things. His gorgeous and elaborate scenery, which, in interest and beauty, so often seems to outweigh by itself all the other constituents of the drama put together, and the comparatively small importance attached by him to the spoken word—even when it is the word of Shakespeare himself—

these are alike instances of a habit of mind which delights far more in expression than in what is expressed. Nothing was more noteworthy in his performance of Antony, in *Antony and Cleopatra*, than the way in which he substituted, for the glowing and passionate utterances of the great Roman, the visible excitements produced by gesture and splendour and pomp. Doubtless the utterances were there, but it was not through them that the dramatic appeal was made; they were totally insignificant; it was only what one saw that mattered. It is hardly an exaggeration to say that Mr Tree is fundamentally a great dumb-show actor, a master of pantomime, and nothing more. And what does this mean? It means that all the subtler effects, all the more delicate presentments of human feeling and human character, are banished from Mr Tree's art. Mere gesture, to produce any impression at all, must be highly generalized, and it must also be grossly exaggerated. One of the great difficulties in acting is to combine dramatic effect with verisimilitude. The actor must never forget that he is acting to an audience, and he must never show the audience that he remembers it. The common fault of uninstructed actors is to give too little attention to their audience, to be too realistic in fact, and thus to fail in dramatic effect. Mr Tree affords an instance of exactly the opposite error. He is so acutely conscious of his audience that he is blind to everything else. In his effort to impress them in the most complete and forcible way, he rejects the use of fine shades and subtle discriminations —the innumerable delicacies of tone and meaning which suggest rather than portray the state of a soul—and he relies solely on such obvious and glaring gesticulations as must be plain to the meanest mind. The result is that he defeats his own object, for the very violence of his action destroys the illusion which it was intended to create. In *Edwin Drood*, for instance, we begin to wonder how it is that the other characters can fail to observe that Jasper

is a conscience-stricken criminal—we see it with such pain-
ful clarity ourselves. Or rather—to put it more accurately
—we see that the part of a conscience-stricken criminal
is being acted by Mr Tree. The truth is that when once
an actor becomes obsessed by his audience he loses his
highest functions. He loses his individuality and his power
of initiative; he becomes an echo of conventions and the
slave of those whom he ought to lead. Audiences like
Mr Tree because they find themselves in him—their own
emphatic, uninspired conceptions of passion and of life.
When he commits a murder on the stage they feel: 'This is
just what a murderer would do.' But a great actor would
make them feel something very different; he would make
them feel: 'A murderer is doing this.' He would lift them
up to his own heights, giving them visions of realities they
had hardly dreamt of, and of mysteries they could never
understand. Mr Tree does not achieve this. He does not
show us life itself, but only the conventional decorations of
life—like the windows of tailors' shops. And so in the long
run his art is unsatisfying. We feel that though it has given
us so much, it has given us nothing that we really desire.

February 1, 1908

The Sicilians

A FEW weeks ago an attempt was made in this column to appraise the acting of Mr Beerbohm Tree, to analyse its nature, and to indicate the principal faults and merits inherent in the species of art of which it is representative. Mr Tree's acting suggests, in more ways than one, a comparison with that of the Sicilian Players, whose vigorous and vivid representations of Italian peasant life are drawing full houses at the Shaftesbury Theatre. Like Mr Tree, these Sicilian actors are primarily concerned with gesticulation; they appeal first and foremost to the eye, and there could be no clearer proof of their mastery of the arts of physical expression than the ease with which they convey to an English audience the developments of a drama spoken in the unfamiliar dialect of Sicily. Indeed, it is impossible not to feel that even Mr Tree, with all his command of gesture and facial play, might learn a good deal upon these matters from the Sicilians. After them, how insignificant and tame appear his most elaborate grimaces, his most melodramatic ravings! He seems to be struggling with his utmost force and skill to achieve effects which come easily, and almost naturally, to Signor Grasso and Signorina Aguglia. And perhaps no English actor or actress, however gifted, could hope to rival, in intensity of physical expressiveness, these hot-blooded children of the South. It is not only that with us the use of gesture, instead of being instinctive and habitual, is a thing to be laboriously learnt; it can hardly be doubted that there is a deeper difference—a difference in nervous organization, in the closeness and swiftness of the correspondence between body and mind. To use the language of science, the Sicilian physique answers far more readily than ours to mental stimuli. They express their feelings, not by the face alone, but by the entire frame; in their climaxes of passion, not a muscle of their bodies remains unmoved; their very feet shiver with emotion; the joints of their thumbs turn backwards, writhing, almost to the wrist. Such intense and extreme manifestations of feeling lie—by the very nature of the case—beyond the reach of a Teutonic pantomimist like Mr Tree.

The superiority of the Sicilians, however, does not depend merely upon the violence of their expressive force; it depends no less on the nature of the feelings which they express. If our analysis was correct, Mr Tree fails to produce truly fine and permanent effects because he attempts to give expression to subtle emotions and complex states of mind by means of crude and obvious gesture. His treatment of Shakespeare affords the clearest instance of this defect, and the same cause tends to make his presentments of modern life stagy and unconvincing. But with the Sicilians the case is very different. The material out of which, so to speak, they weave their acting is something totally dissimilar both to the imaginative intellectuality of Shakespeare and to the refined self-consciousness of the civilized society of today: it is the rough, direct, and primitive existence of the ignorant peasants of the Abruzzi or the simple hill-folk of Sicily. In a word, the emotions with which they deal are precisely those for which vivid physical action is the only appropriate expression. Here are no complexities and hesitations, no hints and delicacies, no gradual transitions of feeling, no subtleties of thought; here everything is simple even to childishness, and straightforward even to brutality. A man flies into a temper with his companion, and immediately slaps his face; the next moment he repents, and kisses him. And in the deeper passions, the greater movements of the soul, there is the same directness and the same swift and violent simplicity. Signorina Aguglia's animalic paroxysms remind one, by sheer force of contrast, of the exquisite refinements of Signora Duse's art, and one begins to wonder how it is that the same race should have produced such opposites. Charles Lamb in his criticism of *The Duchess of Malfi* speaks of the noble spirituality of Webster's tragedy, and points out how that great artist was able 'to move a horror skilfully, to touch a soul to the quick, to lay upon fear as much as it can bear, to wean and weary a life until it is ready to drop'; and adds that 'writers of an inferior genius may "upon horror's head horrors accumulate" but they cannot do this. . . . They mistake quantity for quality . . . their terrors want dignity, their affrightments are without decorum.' It is over this latter province —the province of accumulated horrors—that the Sicilian actress reigns supreme. Doubtless it is not the highest form of tragedy; it is true that her terrors want dignity, and that her affrightments are without decorum; but she has brought these things under the spell of a most potent art, and she has made them the instruments of no mean triumph. The spectacle which she presents of a mind—or should we rather say a body?—given over to the last extremities of unmixed passion—of love, or hatred, or jealousy, or terror, or despair—must send a thrill through the coldest, and impress the most obtuse. It is natural that a superficial criticism should compare Signorina Aguglia with Madame Bernhardt; but in reality any such comparison must be fruitless. Their merits cannot be weighed in the same scales. Madame Bernhardt is before all things a dweller in cities; in her most electric movements she is still civilized; when she is most frenzied she never loses her grace; and at her best she can assume the 'dignity' and the 'decorum' of the grand style itself. Curiously enough, the fundamental situation of the central scene in *Malia* corresponds almost exactly with that of one of the great scenes in *Phèdre*—a scene in which, perhaps, Madame Bernhardt appears at her finest. The subject of both is a woman's declaration of a shameful passion to the object of it. Madame Bernhardt shows us the mind of Racine's heroine, delirious and desperate as it is, yet possessed of a high consciousness, an imaginative grasp of the irony of the situation, and a splendid magnanimity. There is nothing of all this in Signorina Aguglia's Iana—a half-savage creature possessed of devils, torn in pieces by the bare violence of shame and of desire, unsupported by the reticences of convention, and unsoothed by the nobilities of thought. The excess of horror let loose and rampant upon a human being—that is a terrible sight to look upon, perhaps too terrible. Who that saw it did not wish, for a moment, to cry out, so that the dreadful thing might stop?

But, after all, these performances are not all terror; they possess the other ingredient of tragedy—there is pity in them too. It is this that mitigates the hideous crudity of certain passages, and brings some sense of gentleness into the whole. The actors are not cold-hearted dissectors of passion, but men and women who feel and know. No one could doubt that who has seen the look of awful grief in Iana's face as she sits plucking to pieces, with the automatic energy of desperation, the flower she holds in her hand, or who has witnessed the agonized stumblings of the witch in *La Figlia di Jorio*, when she has fallen into her persecutor's power. Enough has been said to show that these actors are by no means the rough-and-ready performers which, from a hasty consideration of the primitive nature of the scenes they depict, they might be supposed to be. Nothing could be further from the truth. They are brilliant and accomplished to a high degree. Signorina Aguglia rises undoubtedly to greatness; and it is rare indeed to see on an English stage an exhibition of such easy power, such consummate mastery of the technique of acting, as is shown by Signor Grasso. The rest of the company err on the side of a too strict adherence to conventional methods, if they err at all. The old men, for instance, are a little too much what everyone would expect old men to be; and the grouping of the minor characters is occasionally over-rigid. But, on the whole, the effect of movement and vitality produced in these pieces is truly amazing. Every actor appears to be overflowing with the vigour of youth. The vivacity and abounding energy of some of the crowded scenes suggest to the mind the great 'Kermesse' of Rubens. The spectator is wonderfully exhilarated; he seems to be drinking, at its very source, of the fountain of life.

February 29, 1908

'L'Art Administratif'

THERE are few pleasanter occupations than the building of castles in the air; and the more elaborate and detailed the construction, the greater the fascination of the work. Mr William Archer and Mr Granville Barker, to whose collaboration we owe an interesting and suggestive volume containing the 'scheme and estimates' for a 'National Theatre',* have thrown themselves with gusto into the task of castle-building, and have produced an airy edifice which for completeness of conception and minuteness of execution it would be difficult to rival. It is clear enough that they have enjoyed their task, and their enjoyment communicates itself straightaway to the reader, who follows with delight wherever the delighted authors choose to lead him. 'Supposing,' Messrs Archer and Barker have in effect said to one another, 'there were put into our hands the sum of £330,000—or, to be on the safe side, let us say £380,000—with which to further the cause of English drama, how should we spend it?' Their book is the answer to the question, and, whatever one may think of the wisdom of this answer, it is impossible to complain of its vagueness. Not content with indicating the main outlines of their scheme, the authors have entered, with scrupulous attention, into the consideration of a vast multitude of details. They are ready with a scheme of decoration for the entrance-hall of their hypothetical theatre; they have drawn up elaborate lists and tables of the repertory of plays to be performed there; they have even gone so far

*A National Theatre: Scheme and Estimates by William Archer and H. Granville Barker. London: Duckworth & Co.

as to create a company of imaginary actors with imaginary names, and to cast them for imaginary parts. When one comes upon a facsimile of the form of application for seats, with directions as to 'returned coupons' and 'postal orders for three shillings', one begins to rub one's eyes, and to wonder whether, after all, an 'airy nothing' so definite and explicit as this can possibly be without a 'local habitation', which somehow or another has escaped one's notice—in the Haymarket or the Strand.

But it would be doing an injustice to the book to suggest that it is nothing more than an ingenious Utopian *jeu d'esprit*. It will be welcome to all who are interested in the welfare of the theatre, if only on the score of the quantity of information which it contains, and the light which it throws on the actual conditions of theatrical work. The improvement of these conditions is the main end which the authors have in view; and the establishment of a 'National Theatre' is, in their opinion, the best and most effectual means for bringing about the desired result. And indeed there can be little doubt that most of the evils of the present system would be—if not remedied—at least ameliorated by their scheme. A theatre in which 'long runs' and 'actor-managers' were alike unknown would offer great advantages both to actors and to dramatists. On the one hand, it would tend to give a much-needed stability to the acting profession, and, on the other, by lessening the risks of dramatic production, it would do away with many of the difficulties and dangers which beset the playwright today. So far every reader of Messrs Archer and Barker's book will find it convincing; but there is a further question, which it nowhere discusses, and upon which the whole of the argument really turns. The advantages of a National Theatre may be great; but what is the price that must be paid for them? Is it not so heavy as to overbalance all the merits of the scheme? One is reminded of the poor wolf in La Fontaine's fable, who was ready to follow the example of the sleek and well-fed dog, until he saw a suspicious something round his companion's neck. What could it be? 'Le collier dont je suis attaché,' explained the dog:

'Attaché? dit le loup; vous ne courez donc pas
Où vous voulez?—Pas toujours; mais qu'importe?
—Il importe si bien que de tous vos repas
     Je ne veux en aucune sorte,
Et ne voudrais pas même à ce prix un trésor.'

And surely the wolf was in the right.

The collar which is round the neck of every National Theatre is the collar of State control—an instrument which is all the more dangerous from its apparent insignificance. It lies there so quietly embedded in the fat folds of the contented animal that it needs the sharp eye of a wolf to detect its presence; and even Mr Archer and Mr Barker, and the squadron of writers from whom they quote, seem to have failed altogether to realize the importance of that fatal word 'attaché'. 'The State,' says Matthew Arnold in a passage which stands as the motto of the present work, 'the nation in its collective and corporate character, does well to concern itself about an influence so important to national life and manners as the theatre,' and the sentiment is re-echoed a hundred times throughout the book. But what does this precisely mean? 'The State shall be my governors, but not my critics,' wrote a greater than Matthew Arnold; and when we are told that the State 'does well to concern itself' with the theatre, or that we must 'organize the theatre', or that we must look forward to 'the recognition of the drama by the State'—whenever we hear such doctrines as these, we shall do well to remember Milton's weighty words. For is it not clear that these doctrines imply by their very nature that the State shall be permitted, and even encouraged, to overstep the functions of government, and to take upon itself the functions of criticism? If a theatre is to be a 'National' theatre in anything but name, it must, in one way or another, come under national control; and whether this control be exercised through the medium of some Government Department under a Secretary of State for Dramatic Affairs or whether—according to the suggestion of Mr Archer and Mr Barker—it be lodged in the hands of a body of public trustees, the same results would inevitably follow. The very names of the bodies to which our castle-builders have given the right of electing trustees are ominous in the extreme—the Universities of Oxford and Cambridge, the Royal Academy, and the London County Council. It would certainly be impossible to name four institutions more representative of the nation, and it would be equally impossible to name any more totally unfitted for having a hand in the management of a theatre. The authors compare the position of their hypothetical trustees with that of the actual Trustees of the British Museum, but the analogy does not hold. For the drama is not a science; it is an art. It is not a dead thing to be pinned down and classified and docketed; it is a living creature, winged and wondrous, hovering inexplicably over magical flowers, and amenable to no laws but those of fancy. Such a phenomenon, it is easy to imagine, would not stay for long in the keeping of public trustees, though doubtless they would be able to furbish up a plausible waxwork imitation to take its place—the art, not of genius, but of mediocrity, the safe, official kind of art, 'l'art administratif', as Renan puts it. Mr Barker in his preface declares that the director of his theatre would be able to include in its repertory such plays as those of Gorky, Ibsen, and D'Annunzio; but surely he is over-sanguine. Who can doubt that a director who ventured upon such bold courses would be very soon brought to book by the Board of Trustees?

And it is not only in its relation to the drama, but in its

relation to the art of acting, that a policy of State criticism must be viewed with dislike and distrust. The establishment of a National Theatre means the establishment of a school of actors and of acting—a school which, by the force of its prestige and the continuity of its tradition, must in the long run assume a predominance over the whole histrionic art of England, with all the claims to orthodoxy and infallibility which such a predominance would inevitably involve. In short, an Academy of Acting would come into existence; but, after all, has our experience of academies been so fortunate as to make us look forward to another with eager hope? The query, as Sir Thomas Browne says, is 'too sad to insist on.' Even in France—under far more favourable conditions—the history of the Comédie Française has been marked by a succession of internecine struggles and intrigues, of monstrous pretensions, and of violent revolts. And in England neither our art nor our character has any natural inclination towards authority. It is hardly an exaggeration to say that there is precisely one way in which to act Molière—the right way—and that all the rest are wrong; but who can limit the number of ways in which it is right to act Shakespeare? The truth is that it is not by means of leading-strings and careful dieting that the English theatre will come to health and strength; no administrative forcing-house will bring it to maturity. It must be allowed, like La Fontaine's wolf, to 'run where it likes'; it must be given the fresh air of freedom. If Mr Archer and Mr Barker could find their £380,000 and would forthwith set up a theatre of their own—a theatre with a repertory and without an acting-manager—they would confer a boon upon our drama which it would be difficult indeed to overestimate. But it must be, without a shadow of a doubt, their own theatre; there must be no trustees.

December 28, 1907